JAMES SINCLAIR

The Millionaire CLOWN

The rules for making it in business,
entrepreneurship and leadership

JAMES SINCLAIR

The Millionaire CLOWN

The rules for making it in business,
entrepreneurship and leadership

MEREO
Cirencester

Mereo Books

1A The Wool Market Dyer Street Cirencester Gloucestershire GL7 2PR
An imprint of Memoirs Publishing www.mereobooks.com

The Millionaire Clown: 978-1-86151-280-2

First published in Great Britain in 2015
by Mereo Books, an imprint of Memoirs Publishing

Copyright ©2015

James Sinclair has asserted hisright under the Copyright Designs and Patents
Act 1988 to be identified as the author of this work.

A CIP catalogue record for this book is available from the British Library.

The address for Memoirs Publishing Group Limited can be found at
www.memoirspublishing.com

The Memoirs Publishing Group Ltd Reg. No. 7834348

The Memoirs Publishing Group supports both The Forest Stewardship Council® (FSC®)
and the PEFC® leading international forest-certification organisations. Our books carrying
both the FSC label and the PEFC® and are printed on FSC®-certified paper. FSC® is the
only forest-certification scheme supported by the leading environmental organisations
including Greenpeace. Our paper procurement policy can be found at
www.memoirspublishing.com/environment

Typeset in 9/15pt Franklin
by Wiltshire Associates Publisher Services Ltd. Printed and bound in Great Britain by
Book Printing UK, Remus House, Coltstfoot Drive, Peterborough, PE2 9BF

CONTENTS

Introduction

PART ONE

Jimbo the Partyman – how it all began

1	The kid who liked to show off	P. 1
2	Entrepreneur in short trousers	P. 7
3	Building a grown-up business	P. 13

PART TWO

Success – and how to achieve it

THE RULES OF SUCCESS

1	Know who you are and where you're going	P. 21
2	Write down your goals	P. 34
3	OST – objective, strategy and tactics	P. 38
4	People – finding them, working with them, developing them and keeping them	P. 42
5	Think BIG, act SMALL – even when you're BIG	P. 55
6	Learn how to raise finance	P. 64
7	Understand marketing, and why it matters	P. 78
8	Become a brand to create trust	P. 93
9	How multiple revenue streams make your business stronger	P. 99
10	Why residual income is the fandabbydozy of business goals	P. 104
11	Learn basic accounting and cash flow	P. 108
12	If you're the smartest person in the room, you're in the wrong room	P. 112
13	Consistency, consistency and more consistency	P. 118
14	Build a network, and keep networking	P. 124
15	Buy a failing business and make it great	P. 127
16	Compete on experience, not price	P. 132
17	Seize opportunities	P. 138

INTRODUCTION

Hi everyone, and congratulations on buying this book. It's a big fat congratulations, because I do believe we will have some fun together and learn a ton of stuff to use in life from my experience of 15 years in business, starting at the age of 14.

I wrote this little book for those who want to be at the top – people who own or run a business, or are about to start the adventure of running one. More than anything, it's intended to help you with some little nuggets to get you off on a super-successful life in business.

Recently I met one of the greatest female entrepreneurs I have ever met. Did she own a business? No, she was the head of a school, but boy was she an inspiration to me. She ran the place as if it was a business, and her entrepreneurial spirit and different way of thinking have made it one of the best schools in the country. Entrepreneurs are no longer just business owners - they are all around us, making a difference in our ever-changing world.

I have spent a year asking myself - should I really write a book? Am I too young? Well, now I have decided to get off my bottom and get on with it. It's all about implementation, because I strongly believe that once you have decided to do something you just need to do it. That's what makes people great entrepreneurs. As you will discover over these pages, I get things done. A common factor that separates OK entrepreneurs from great entrepreneurs is that they don't just get great ideas - they then get the ideas done

What's a millionaire?

Don't be fooled by the title of this book. Many people are millionaires on paper and to be fair, that means toffee to me. The title is to prove a point - that I'm a clown who's done good because I learned along the way and put what I learned into action - simple. In the last six months I have doubled the size of my business (again). If I really wanted to, I could sell up and go and spend the rest of my life lying on a beach - but that doesn't mean I can lay my hands on a ton of cash or drive off in a new Ferrari any time I want to. That's not what being an entrepreneur means – not in the real world, not in my world anyhow. The money I have is for investing – for the next project.

This is my story so far. It all started when I was just 14. It's taken a lot of blood, sweat and tears, and a lot of love and laughter. Why have I written it? Because I know there is nothing all that special about me. I am just an ordinary Essex bloke who happens to have a massive drive for success and getting things done.

I say this again and again - any man or woman could do the same. All you need is a lot of hard work, and you will be shocked how much luck you get when you work hard and learn some rules of business along the way. I hope my book will inspire you to create something of your own, something truly magical.

Easy it isn't, but once you get a little traction and learn a little, the rewards are worth it. Remember things change all the time. We have economic downturns, social media trends, booms and busts, new ways to market, new trends – no doubt a new fancy phrase for something new will have been invented before this book's been out more than a few weeks. It's a fast-changing world. But if you've got the business-building bug and you are determined to succeed and refuse to stay down when your get the knocks, you can do it, despite all the crap excuses people come out with. Blaming the economy and the government are just excuses. For me personally, it's all about deciding what you want to do and getting going. For most of my business life I've been trading in a recession.

So let's get going, let's get some stuff implemented, let's gets some work done!

That first million

Lots of books about how to get rich have been written by people who have never run successful businesses themselves. This book, if you follow the advice in it properly, could help you to get from zero to a million in a few years. It's not a manual or a how-to-do-it guide, more a set of guidelines which will help you to find your way to success the way I did. I'm not a business graduate or a master of economic theory – I don't know everything. I'm aware that as with all entrepreneurs, my success has come despite making a few mistakes along the way. No doubt I will make others, and quite frankly – bring 'em on, baby!

So why, at the tender age of 29 with my business still young, did I decide to tell the story of my journey on paper? Because I didn't want to wait until I had forgotten what these early years have been like. By the time I'm 60, chances are I'll be looking back at the early days with rose-tinted spectacles. I'll probably have forgotten some of the vital details which made all the difference. Right now, they are still fresh in my mind. Fact is, over the last 14 years I've seen as much unhappiness and strife as success. It's been fun, but it's been hard, and I don't want to forget that.

I'm hoping the next five or ten years will be a little easier than the last five or ten. After the first 10 years in business, given a measure of success, it ought to get easier – you've made your cash, so you have something to work with. You can set up a second business if you want to, and a third, knowing you can always fall back on the first if you need to. You haven't just accumulated cash – you've gained experience, knowhow, contacts, friends and most of all TRUST. Once you've got your first million in the bank, believe me, the bank manager is going to pay attention when you tell him you want his help. Also you will trust yourself and your abilities if you want to be a great entrepreneur.

The business-building bug

Building businesses is like a bug, and it can't be cured. Once you've caught it, you can't get rid of it. It's a good bug. It can drive you on to success. BUT – you need to control it. Otherwise you risk damaging and losing those things in life you can't replace – your family, loved ones and friends. Too many rich people end up lonely, having lost people who really mattered to them because all they could think about was the money or the business.

So you'll need to learn to set limits. Sometimes it's better to take a small risk by putting a big business deal on hold for a few hours than to take a bigger one – the risk of losing the love and respect of a child, because you didn't make it to their birthday party. Sadly, I have seen this happen many times.

Because of my difficult start in life I have probably missed the most important opportunities – and I don't mean business opportunities. I regret that to this day. I can't stress this enough – money on its own does not make you happy. In fact, if you damage your personal and emotional life, you will damage your business as well - guaranteed.

They say you learn by mistakes, and that is so true. Never, ever, imagine that just because you've had a good run up until now you know it all, and everything you touch is guaranteed to turn to gold. I have nearly lost it all myself, two or three times. Risk is unavoidable. What's essential is to understand and manage the risk, so if it all goes pear-shaped you're in a position to bounce back. Risks are part of the game. Just make sure they are calculated ones.

Along the way you will have some hurdles – big hurdles that most people just wouldn't be able to jump. If I hadn't found a way of jumping them, I wouldn't be writing this.

This book will give you a little insight into some of the challenges of a successful business - how to cope with hundreds of staff, frighteningly big loans, stupid rules and red tape. How to handle investors or banks, how to invest your cash, calculate risks, manage cash flow issues.

It's tough at the start

Above all I just want to say – look, business is hard, but you're not alone, most people start on a rocky road. I know what it's like to wake up in the morning feeling you're in such a mess that you might as well pack it all in. I want to make you feel that it will get better. I always remember the late, great Steve Jobs saying that the reason most business owners give up is because they are sane.

If you haven't realised it by now, I'm a bloke who says what he thinks. But I'm not a nasty bastard and I certainly don't walk around as if I owned Wall Street. I tell it like it is, in my own slightly comical way, with a little love and a sprinkle of magic.

I wanted to dedicate this book to the memory of my Mum, Mandy, and my Granddad, Del Boy. Sadly I lost both of them within three months of each other when I was 18. That was hard to cope with. They would both have got a real kick out of this, seeing all the things that we have created. Granddad was my driver when I started out – I didn't want a driver because I thought I was royalty, I needed one, because I was only 15 years old and had no other way of getting to work to run my first business effectively. Of course I paid him, though not very well I'm afraid. I think about them both all the time, and yes I do talk to them and ask for help. They never answer directly, but somehow when I've spoken to them, things seem to work out.

This adventure has taught me the nasty side of business as well as the good stuff, the stuff you can't learn unless you do it. As I said earlier, I wanted to write this book now, not when I'm old and have everything paid off and I'm fat and ugly and ready to retire (don't worry - I never will retire and I don't think I'll ever be fat either. Ugly – well, that's a matter of opinion).

You see, the nature of the beast is that usually as a business grows it gets easier. Banks, suppliers and customers love established businesses, and so they should. Businesses are like people - the older they get the wiser they get, as long as, in my opinion, the entrepreneur at the top keeps learning and investing to make himself the best leader, listener and make-things-happen person he or she can be. I am writing this book as part of my self-development, my drive to be better, for me and my team. Entrepreneurs are very special people - they create employment. Often they fail, not because they don't work hard enough but because they have not learned the rules. Yet every now and then a kid genius turns things upside down and beats the establishment.

Kisses and cuddles

The beginning is hard, specially getting the capital to grow. I hear many business people say that you don't need money to start a business. In some cases that's true, but because you managed to do it that way doesn't mean to say it's the right way – it may just have been the only way. I needed half a million quid to take my business to the next stage, which is difficult when you're 20.

We talk a lot about giving our customers a 'cuddle' at Partyman, and this book will be the 'cuddle', the caring advice, that could help you get through those times. That's why over the coming pages you will share my views of business and put them into nice little bite-size chunks. This advice should be simple and easy for you to grasp, just like a good business - forget that, just like a GREAT business.

Along with the cuddle, don't forget the KISS - Keep It Simple Stupid, a phrase which originally came out of the US Navy. It summarises a great approach to a successful business. I hate complicating things, so I'm not going to complicate this book.

My little lessons about how my small business got to be bigger and then a lot bigger, and how I overcame my troubles, could help you. You don't have to follow everything I say as it may not all work for you, but these are the nuggets that have helped me.

Plan ahead

You also need to plan ahead for when you get bigger and work out what you'll do with all the people you'll employ - the cash in the bank, the succession planning, decisions to sell or go national. Things can happen very quickly. Believe me, planning at the start what you want to look like in 10 years' time can help massively. You don't have to make an elaborate business plan, but you do need to start with an OBJECTIVE - and you need to appreciate all the mistakes you make and know how to learn from them on the way. You will be amazed how many businesses don't have a plan or an objective (more on this later).

Business is tough. In most cases it takes years to create what I call proper profit, and to me profit is not what your accountants tell you it is, it's what you can take out of the business. You need to learn when you can take money out without starving the business of the cash it needs to function.

The owner gets the annual profit to reinvest or keep, but on top of this you will have built a business that is worth something, should you want to sell. Profit grows in a business as its value grows. Imagine the value of a 10-year-old business that makes a £300k net profit every year.

I want this book to be an inspiration. Failure and success are so close sometimes. I have nearly lost all I have spent in time and money on at least three occasions. Sometimes, if you have the growth bug bad, you begin to think you are always right and everyone else is always wrong. Being a good listener and knowing which advice is right is a key skill, if you want to be an entrepreneur who moves mountains.

The key to getting ahead is knowing which advice is right and which is wrong. I often plough ahead with an idea, but then if my staff tell me they have a better one I am always ready to listen and go with theirs instead.

The wide view

I like to think a successful entrepreneur is like a great family doctor. You must never become a specialist or a consultant in any one area without knowing about the others – you need the wide view. Being the 'business GP' who knows the key essentials about all the aspects of a business - sales, marketing, accounts, operations, customer service, HR, banking, general economics, public speaking, planning, finance, health and safety - is vital. When you need specialist help, you need to know where to turn to find the experts who have the right knowledge and experience, just like a really good doctor who knows that if a situation is too complicated for him he knows a go-to specialist doctor who can treat the condition. It's very similar in business. At first these people will simply be friends. Later they will be your suppliers, investors and trading partners. Eventually they will be members of your own team.

The reason you must keep that broad view is that you need to know a little about every aspect of the business without becoming too focused on any particular one. Your time and energy should be spent investing in growth and the bigger picture. You need to be working ON the business, not IN it - you are a business owner, not an operator, worker or manager. If you are working in the business, your business will never see real opportunity or progress for you and the team. If you stick at the same treadmill every day, how can you get new leads, suss the latest trends or see what the competition is up to?

Of course, you may start as a specialist. If you start a business as an engineer, for example, and get a first contract that keeps you in the workshop, it'll be hard to go out looking for contracts two, three and four. You're going to have to tear yourself away from what you know and let someone else fulfil the first contract while you concentrate on the bigger picture. But don't just leave poor old Fred to slave away in the workshop while you go swanning around winning new business – respect and value the skills of the specialists, and show them they are respected. At the same time Fred needs to respect you, to know that you're out there working just as hard as he is, for the future of the business. Usually a good entrepreneur or business owner learns this very quickly.

Any business owner, leader or entrepreneur who has hit success quickly learns that they are an entrepreneur first, not a worker or manager, so anyone who comes out with that old line 'if you want a job done properly, do it yourself' will only get so far, because there comes a point when you're running a growing business when doing it yourself is no longer possible. You need to get systems in place so you don't have to.

This book will cover the key subjects which I have learned you must master to succeed with your business. Everything I have written is based on what I have learned myself - by actually doing it.

So let's get doing it.

PART ONE

Jimbo the Partyman – how it all began

One

THE KID WHO LIKED TO SHOW OFF

I didn't like my childhood, not one bit. I was a spotty, gangly kid, and so thin I could fall down a drain. I couldn't wait to leave home – in fact I can remember at the age of 13 or 14 wishing for the years to fly past faster so I could get to adulthood. My dad had left home at 15, and I was planning to follow his example as closely as possible.

My mum, Mandy, and my dad, Ian, were a fairytale couple. They met working at school when they were both just 15 and fell in love for life. They were very happy, and had great jobs. They owned their own house, something none of their friends achieved, and moved three times in the early years of their marriage. Mum had a lively, fun personality, as does my dad, although they were very different. Dad has a good brain for money and an acute business mind, though not like mine – he wouldn't share my enjoyment in looking after hundreds of staff. But Mum loved people and they loved her. A mixture of their personalities is definitely within me.

I was born on the 14th of June 1985. By the time I had arrived in the world, it had all started to go wrong for Mum. While she was still pregnant with me, she was diagnosed with MS. On doctor's orders, she was not told at first, in case it affected the pregnancy.

When I was born, my mum was as high as a kite with hormone imbalances, and needed looking after as much as I did. My dad told me a story recently which I thought was hilarious, though it was sad at the same time. Dad was working shifts for the *Daily Mail*, and he came home from work to find a stranger in the house looking after me. My mum had gone out to hit the town and left me with a babysitter who she didn't even know.

In the end a psychiatrist put me and Mum in a specialist hospital to help her bond with me and get her hormones under control. By this time, she had found out that she had MS and was in a bad way. Imagine being in your twenties with a new baby and knowing that in a few years' time you might not be able to walk!

MS varies enormously in the speed of onset, and Mum was unlucky. She deteriorated very quickly and as the illness increased its grip on her body she was soon dragging one leg.

Fast forward a little, and Mum and Dad had divorced. I did live with Mum in Rainham for a while, but she went downhill really fast. She was soon getting so bad that one day I had to call an ambulance for her because she collapsed and burned herself trying to cook our dinner. I was only three. As you can imagine, this was a real wake-up call for her.

Mum then had to call Dad to come and look after me, so I went to live in Elm Park with Dad and his sister, my Aunt Elizabeth, or 'Aunty Lizzy Bit', as I called her. I can't imagine what that must have been like for Mum, having to give up her son to the man she had divorced. It would have taken real balls to make that call, knowing that a horrific illness was taking over her body at a rate of knots. And the sadness and loneliness didn't stop there.

I think these early situations are the reason I am so wary of family and love letting you down. It really got to me as a kid. To this day I still can't remember ever having a cuddle from my mum, because as the illness got worse she lost the use of her arms. I think it's more cruel when you still have the use of your brain but not your body. You know what you want to do, you know where you want to go, but your body says no. As my lovely Nan always says, 'health is wealth'. You'd better believe it, folks – we need to look after that body we all go around in.

Dad and Aunty Lizzy Bit looked after me for a couple of years, and I have such fond memories of those times. I suppose Lizzy had become like a mum to me, and I loved her lots. However, she then met a new man and she went on to have (and still does have) a happy life with him. My dad then met his current partner, Jill, and they married when I was five. We moved to Brentwood when I was seven - I remember hating that because I loved my school and friends, and it seemed a million miles away, although it only took 20 minutes to get there. Funny how kids measure distance.

From this point on I did not enjoy my childhood. I felt it lacked love, and that's the one thing a child needs more than anything. If kids don't have it they build walls, and I certainly built walls.

I was scared of my dad at times, but his sometimes hard approach has given me a great grounding for business, and to be honest I didn't like Jill very much when I was little - what kid does like his step-parents? I always missed my mum and Nan, who I got to see every other weekend. Funny, because now I have a great relationship with Jill, as I do with my dad.

I always wondered why I was never cuddled and never heard the 'L' word – love. My mum was in a wheelchair by the time I was five and I saw her only at weekends. As her illness got worse, she lost the use of the good leg she had as well as her arms. What love I did get was from my dear Nan. More on this wonderful lady later. To this day I can't remember receiving proper love or cuddles during my childhood. I remember going round friends' houses and thinking wow - look at this family, they LIKE their kids, I want some of that!

I tell you all this to set the scene and understand why I am the way I am. It's often said that serial business leaders and entrepreneurs are a little removed from normal life, and I think that's true. Some even say they are psychopaths – though that may be going a bit far - in most cases!

Learning was never my strong point as a child. I did OK at school, but never pushed myself. School did teach me how to deal with adults and wriggle out of situations, but on the whole I thought it was a waste of time - life is what teaches you. I started to learn the second I left, and I have never stopped.

Unless you know what you want to do in life, I still think university is a waste of time. You have to know what the objective is and why you're doing it and getting into all the debt that goes along with it. If you want to be a doctor or a lawyer it's a different matter of course, but I don't have much time for people who go to university just for something to do and to put off the day they have to start work. You will soon learn through these pages that in my view, time is the most precious commodity we all have. If you could sell time, you would instantly be the richest man in the world. As Benjamin Franklin said, there are only two things we can all be certain of in life - death and taxes. So use time wisely. It's worth more than all the riches in the world.

I got the urge to build my own business very early on. I was the kid who sold sweets at school, took Saturday jobs and worked every hour I could to make a bit of money. My best friend Mark had started doing mobile discos for kids at weekends, and he was out every weekend earning £20 an hour - I thought that seemed pretty good, as most kids would have been happy to earn £2 an hour then. But I didn't want to be a disc jockey, and I began to wonder what I could do instead.

From an early age I was the kid who loved acting and performing - drama was the subject I excelled in at school, and making people laugh and doing impressions were right up my street. I was quite good,

4

if I say so myself. I got to be quite a pro at doing all the top politicians and school teachers, but I really excelled at Jim Carrey.

It was at my little sister Abby's birthday party that a light bulb suddenly switched on. I was 14, maybe 15, and she was five years old. Our family had organised a children's entertainer for the party. So did he inspire me by his routine? No - he was useless! To me it was just old-fashioned shite. I knew I could jazz it up and make it better, but everyone loved him just the same. I couldn't work it out, but I realised it was a new market and a new industry, and it presented a real opportunity.

As I said, I had by now discovered a love for drama and entertaining. I had even started going to weekend stage schools. This was the first thing I had found that I could do well, and I really enjoyed it, as I do to this day. I LOVE entertaining, being the centre of attention and making people laugh. It gave me a release from my family problems and a chance to show off and use my naturally extrovert personality. I thought to myself, I can do a hell of a lot better than this bloke – and he was being paid £100, just for entertaining a few kids for an hour and a half.

By the time Abby's party was over, I knew what I wanted to do with my life - at least, at first. I started to hatch a plan for an entertainment agency. The name I chose was Sinclair Entertainments (yes I know, dull and unimaginative - I was only 15 though and thought it sounded grown up, so cut me some slack). I quickly changed my strategy and went on to work on my objective to create a national brand that families would love. Stage 1 was to create the UK's biggest and best children's birthday party provider.

I should add that I moved out of Dad's house when I was 18 and went to live with Nan. Sadly I lost Mum in January 2003 and Granddad had died in the November a few months before– he was in in a terrible car accident. It was an awful three months, but these things do toughen you up.

Mum and Granddad just got to see the start of all this stuff I was doing, and they would have got a real kick to see what I've achieved. I'm sure they are looking down and loving it.

All this taught me to be happy, not to give up, to stay positive and enjoy life. It's short, and we need to do what good we can while we are here.

Thanks Granddad, for driving me round to all the countless gigs and shows all round London and Essex. If you hadn't taught me the roads and constantly said 'well done' and 'fantastic job son', I don't think I would have the positive outlook on life you had, and I certainly wouldn't have got going so quickly. I hope I can be a great Granddad just like you in the future.

Two

ENTREPRENEUR IN SHORT TROUSERS

I was 15 when I got the work bug. I started with a paper round – in fact I had FOUR paper rounds. Not surprisingly I often mucked up, and sent papers to the wrong houses. I soon realised that it was too much like hard work, but it got me started.

It was the paper rounds that taught me you can only make so much money with your hands. If I wanted to double my takings I would have to double my time, until inevitably the day ran out. At 15 I learned this straight away - that time is the most valuable of all assets. Indeed, as I tell all my staff and the people I talk to, time is the one commodity you can't replace. You can lose money, staff, dare I say it even love, but you can replace them eventually. You can never get time back.

I set a goal of earning £40,000 a year and owning a house by the time I was 20, and by heck I was determined to do it. I carried on with the paper rounds and soon moved on to the classic dodge of selling sweets in the playground. It was great - buy them low, sell them high. People would come to me not because of the sweets but because I was funny. I would chuck in a comedy impression of one of the teachers to get the sale. People would say, 'Sinclair, do Mrs So and So', and I would do the impression and get the sale with a smile.

People started to come to me for the impressions as much as the sweets.

I soon realised that humour and selling go hand in hand, and in a funny way maybe it was the beginning of my mantra - that if you provide an experience in what you sell people remember you, but are willing to pay for your services - and pay more! Remember this and write it down 20 times - learn to compete on experience, not price. Much more on this later.

I negotiated discounted rates with the paper shop I did my newspaper rounds for, and carefully dodged the teachers at school, knowing that if I got caught the business would be finished. I wonder how many successful people started their business lives like that?

There were three of us who traded at the school, and eventually of course we got caught and that was the end of the road. Time to look for something new. I continued with the paper rounds, but the £5 a day profit from sweets needed replacing with a safer income.

Enter the food and beverage training. At weekends and school holidays I worked in a greasy spoon café and pizza takeaway for an incredible character called Colin Whymark, who was the only actual boss I have ever had. He taught me loads. Colin was a business owner and manager who tried to break out. He was running his café by day and a pizza shop by night. He was good with customers and networked with local big business people, and he was always dealing with other jobs when he could.

I loved the café. We had big builders and crazy characters in there. My favourite regular was a guy who thought he was Adolf Hitler. He had even shaped his moustache to look like that of the Nazi dictator. To this day I mimic some of the ways Colin would deal with things. He had a way of telling you off and getting things done with a smile. He was a hilarious man with an Italian look about him, small and as round as a pound, and he had huge bushy eyebrows.

THE MILLIONAIRE CLOWN

Businessmen like Colin are a dying breed. Nowadays local businesses need to appear service-led and professional, with a key detail offering that big business struggles to deliver – either that or it needs to be saying, 'Hey big nasty corporate, look at me! It will take you two years and 400 board meetings to do what I can do in four minutes'.

I was only 15 when I created my first brand and my first business - Jimbo The Partyman. Jimbo was, and is, a hugely outrageous entertainer for children and families who appeals to adults too, just as a Disney Pixar animated movie does. Inventing Jimbo was my first lesson in branding and recognition. If you can build a brand that's trusted and loved, you've made it - but more on this later. It was also simpler and easier to remember than my first attempt, Sinclair Entertainments. People got it straight away - I was a kids' entertainer appealing to kids, where previously I had been a kids' entertainer with a professional name that fitted with a wedding crowd. The point I learned here was not to just use your name, it's lazy. Put some thought into what your objective is, and who you want to be to your customers.

I used the money I earned working for Colin to buy props and DJ equipment for my magic shows and entertaining. I started entertaining at local parties in Brentwood, for schools and beaver and cub groups. My big break came when I met a lady called Denise Austin, who put me in touch with an established local entertainer called Craig Gallimore. He was in his late twenties, a bald guy from Stoke on Trent, so he was a real novelty in the chav world of Essex. But Craig was good, really good, and he had a full diary. I was in awe of him and his personality - in a way he was my first mentor. He helped me out and passed on work to me that he couldn't handle. In return I would give him a booking fee.

The Jimbo act which I do to this day was my start in life. At 18, I was doing 10 to 15 parties a week. I used puppets, magic, balloons and some extraordinary props of my own, like motorised granny scooters with giant water pistols attached and balloons I would climb into. I would also ship the world's best magic tricks to my parties - all to reach my objective. I was going to do all I could to becoming the busiest and the best, never the cheapest.

To this day I invest time and money in putting on the best show I can. I turned the stupid idea of wearing waistcoats and bow ties upside down - I jazzed it up and changed the way it had always been done. I went for shorts, cool trainers, trendy hair and a full PA system with headset mics and clear colours that kids could recognise. Purple and yellow were my choice, and to this day they are still our brand colours.

I did all I could to create an experience - even my van was fully signwritten with a talking PA system, flashy lights and a horn that played music as I arrived. That's right - as I passed people in the street or arrived at parties I would talk to people from the cab of my van – I'd already learned to compete on experience, not price.

I was soon flat out working as Jimbo the Partyman, and at the age of 16 I had to leave Colin and the café. I started doing parties for people and schools really cheap – in fact that was the one and only time I have ever competed on price, simply because no one had experienced what I had to offer, so I had to get my foot in the door. I was putting myself out for £20 an hour, which got my name out there - as it was so cheap, people were willing to risk the money and give me a chance. As soon as I could, I started charging the right price for the experience I was delivering.

By the time I'd been going 18 months and was 17 years old, I was fully booked every weekend for a year ahead. By then I was turning over £500-£1000 a week. I was hyperactive and over the top and I always tried to entertain the whole family, not just the little ones, so the parents came in and watched, and they laughed along with their kids.

It was a fun time, and it helped me to build a great relationship with my family on my mum's side. I was living with my Nan and Granddad at weekends, and we travelled far and wide, across the whole of Essex and London. I became a real navigator, but it took me five tries to pass my driving test. In fact I only finally managed to pass after Granddad died.

By the time I was 17, Jimbo The Partyman was all I could think about. I threw everything into building my Jimbo business. By the time I was 19 I couldn't do it all myself and I had employed my first entertainer, as well as a part-time secretary, Jean, who worked with me in Nan's spare bedroom – yes, Nan put up with a lot. I used her garage and put up a shed to accommodate all the stock the business needed.

Around this time I started a side business selling toys to newsagents – that was a valuable early lesson to me, because I soon found out it was a waste of time. I did persuade around 30 stores to be my customers, and I would fill a suitcase and show my wares to them, but it was all about price, so it was impossible to make any money. Quite a learning experience – it certainly reminded me about my rule to compete on experience, never on price. This little failure taught me that some businesses are solely going to compete on price and not experience – I had found myself trying to compete in a totally price-led business, and I wanted out.

I worked seven days a week, and in five years I didn't take more than five days off. At night I would do mobile discos, and during the day I would run the office. Then when 3 pm came I would pack my clown van full of props for my after-school birthday parties, while at weekends I'd do four children's parties a day. Sometimes I was doing 18 parties in a week. Things kept growing, and by the age of 20 I had 10 full-time entertainers and face-painters, as well as an events company which I called the Partyman Company. I was now supplying big companies with corporate entertainment such as fun days, DJs and magicians. We do it to this day, on a bigger scale now, but we still do little Johnny's party.

When I was 19 I started my agency for children's entertainment, so I started to train new entertainers my ways of doing this new style of entertainment, by letting them shadow me, heck even move in with me. Recruiting was always difficult because I strove for the best. What I was looking for was to create 'mini mes', because my customers trusted what I did, so I needed to replicate. I would audition at drama schools and tirelessly interview to get the best. This was my first insight into passive income, where business makes money for you without using your hands and doing everything in your own time.

Early on I was lucky enough to recognise my weakness and not do things that bored me, so I needed people to do the stuff I didn't want to do or wasn't good at. The first person I took on was Jean, to do my paperwork and make sure it was efficient and proper so that I was free to concentrate on sales and look for new opportunities. I learned very quickly to keep on top of the business and not get sidetracked into anything mundane or boring. Other people love paperwork, so let them do it. I hate it, and to this day I never get involved with it. Use the skills you are good at. Admin is easy to buy in, so buy it in. It's your job to focus on the business, to keep concentrating on the big picture. That's the only way to success.

TOP TIP

As a business owner, you must never forget that one of your main objectives is to get and keep customers.

Three

BUILDING A GROWN-UP BUSINESS

By the time I was 19 I had saved enough from my entertaining to buy a house in Brentwood, Essex, and by the time I was 20 I had another, in Rayleigh. I had to live on thin air at times to save up for the deposits on these, but I knew I needed property to achieve long-term success. The following year I rented the Brentwood house out and moved into the Rayleigh one. More later about my pension planning and property dealings.

At first I lived with Leanne, my girlfriend at the time, but we were very young and it didn't last. After she moved out, Aaron, my right-hand man and first full-time member of staff, moved in. I met Aaron at a party I did for David Lloyd Health and Leisure Centres. He was the team leader for kids' activities and we hit it off straight away. We agreed on everything, and still do – well, most of the time! Aaron was great with customers and had the same outlook as me. I quickly offered him a job.

Aaron soon nicknamed the Rayleigh house Partyman Towers, and that's what we still call our head office. He and I shared the same objective - he wanted to work for a business that was going places, one that wanted to become a national brand. I offered him £1000 a month plus free bed and board, and we were away. To this day we have never had so much fun.

Aaron still runs everything. He works IN the business and I work ON the business. We have a perfect relationship, and both respect the other's job to make things happen and not to get in each other's way.

One of the most vital elements in business success is having a manager who can understand and develop your ideas and see them through. As the entrepreneur you are the innovator, the ideas man, but you cannot make your vision work without your manager, and the manager will get bored without the entrepreneur. It's like husband and wife - the two have to go hand in hand. As the company grows you will take on more people to run the business for you, but Aaron is special. He's the same age as me and he has now been my best friend, and as the Mafia would say my *consigliere* (right-hand man), for a decade. For a 29-year-old to have found his number one so early on is unusual and I've had him by my side for 10 years. It's been a real key to our success as a company. To this day I run all the big decisions past Aaron before anyone else. I get great advice, love and friendship all rolled into one - how fab is that? I love the man and luckily I know he loves me.

Aaron and I moved in together at Partyman Towers and started to develop our entertainment agency. We added other business lines and constantly talked about growing the business. We lived, slept and breathed Partyman.

In the early days I started buying in services like accounts. Vicki was my first accountant and she kept us organised and ready for the big plan to come, Partyman World.

The house in Rayleigh was perfect. There was room to park seven cars and we had a huge granny annexe, in which we had a meeting table and four desks. Those years were some of the happiest of my life. We moved in another guy, Luke, who worked for us part-time, and built a strong business. Right from the early days, we got to be known around Essex for being THE party entertainer providers. Then it spread to London, Hertfordshire, Kent and beyond.

Partyman Towers was fun, really great fun. All we did was laugh loud and work hard. If we had entered it in an award scheme for the best place to work, we would have won. We would imagine we were bigger than we were. When calls were put through Aaron, Luke and I used to give ourselves pretend names so people didn't think they were talking to the people they were actually booking. It was so funny - Aaron was Russell Love and I was Tom Smith. We made our own on-hold music for customers to listen to while they were waiting for the next pretend person to be connected. We even pretended we had an accounts team, but in reality it was just me with different voices. What we did, which I loved, was to put on our phone system a welcome message with a difference. It went: 'Welcome to the Partyman Company. Press 1 to talk to a baboon, press 2 to hear a funny noise, 3 to hear a joke...' Memorable, and right on brand. I still love these little touches that make us who we are.

In the early days of the granny annexe we would work in our pants and dressing gowns till midday, and I would trundle off to the kitchen to make bacon and chicken sandwiches. We would hit the phones all day long. We honestly thought even then that we were going to become millionaires in 12 months' time.

Aaron blossomed with me and I blossomed with him. To be fair, we taught each other a lot. I was ruthless and on the money, while he was more laid back and cautious. He learned a lot and added an ingredient to the mix that really made our company tick.

From the day Aaron started, I dropped the 'I' word and became 'we'. Even now people question me and say 'who's we?' when I am talking about the strangest of things. For example, 'We're going to build this here and we are going to change this' really means I am going to do this, but my team, my family, are so important and so vital to business success, especially if you want to grow as we do.

We were a small business, in reality, and I have always been a goal man. I write my goals down and plan for targets to be achieved by a certain date. I get close to depression if they are not achieved and really punish myself if that happens. It's stupid, and something I need help for.

I always worry that time will run out and not enough has been done – it's a peculiar thing, I just want to do so much with the business and my life. Above all I hate wasting time, and I mean HATE it. I hate it when others waste time too.

Only recently I have started to think about quality 'me time' and all the years I lost for myself while building the business, something anyone who reads this must pick up. You must create time for you and yours. It's difficult, because you want to create a great business, and it can consume you. Try at all costs not to let this happen. It has always consumed me, because it's like a drug. I just find it such fun, and I always want that fun to get bigger.

Once we had set up our entertainment business, we started to look at our own events and began to buy bouncy castles and fun equipment so we could do family fun days, school fetes and staff company reward days. This was great, as companies would hire us in to do massive family fun days to say 'thank you' to their teams and Partyman would provide it all - entertainment, equipment, decor and theming. This gave us a new revenue stream. It was highly lucrative if you could get enough booked in - and we did!

By the time I was 20 we were providing work for massive companies like BP and Ikea. I remember us landing a corporate job which paid £23,000 for one day's work - it was one of the biggest self-belief moments in my career. I was determined that we would get the job booked, and after we got one in the bag we steadily booked more and more.

THE MILLIONAIRE CLOWN

We built our events company very quickly. It was doing so well and we were eager to get new event equipment to hire out, so we decided to take a trip to the Leisure Show at the NEC. I had an ambition to open an indoor play centre by the time I was 21, so we thought we could look into that as well while we were away. But getting the capital to do it was difficult. I had two houses and a good income, but the money was all going on running the company and equipment investment, so it was at the back of my mind and not really a possibility just then.

In fact, what was supposed to be a two-day trip turned into five, and that's how the story of us becoming a 'bigger' company began, in September 2006. That week we drove to Birmingham, Liverpool and London looking at play centres. When we had seen the play area manufacturers, we decided we just wanted to do it no matter what. We were going to open a play centre with a difference.

Nine months later it was up and running. I was 20 when the planning started. Somehow I got together half a million pounds (more about raising finance in chapter 5) and rented a huge 15,000 square foot warehouse which we turned into a commercial kitchen, storage, offices, restaurant and play venue for the children of Basildon in Essex. We went from turning £150,000 a year to a million in a very short time. I was 20 and had staff, rent, VAT and PAYE to worry about and I was running these complicated operations. We had no idea really, but we were driven - and still are - by common sense and tight cash controls.

It helped that marketing and PR came easily to me, and for a 20-year-old Aaron was amazingly good at the operational side. Somehow I knew that the place was going to be a success, and it was. On our first day we took nearly £6000. The day before we opened we had nothing, no reception or toilets, but we managed. We moved fast. We improved quickly and we've kept on improving. We always strive to be better, every day.

That 'Partyman' name really stuck. When we built our first play centre, that's what we called it - Partyman World. Now we have four more of them, as well as five play centres, four day nurseries, three laser arenas, an online shop, an events business and a farm park. The business turns over £8 million and makes money.

You don't grow from £100k turnover to £8 million in seven years without a few problems, both business and personal. It's a beast that consumes you, and you can lose touch with normal life.

So how does a 20-something-year-old keep raising cash to grow his business? At first I had loans, but as the financial crisis hit, it was harder to get the cash together, especially as my business kept needing high capital expenditure to grow. I found ways to do this – I'll go into more detail in chapter 6 about raising finance.

I had struggled to get cash for growth, so I used the cash the business was generating - a cardinal sin and a dangerous way to play the game of building a business. Unfortunately, if the banks won't lend you seldom have a choice, if you don't have millions already. Playing this game nearly lost me it all - in fact I had to put one of my companies into administration. This taught me a great deal. Since then I have become known for taking failing businesses, stamping them with my brand and turning them round. Because I had had to put one of my businesses into administration, this taught me the ins and outs of failure and learning how to deal with it. In fact I have now bought and turned around many bad businesses and I will continue to do so. If you can take over from someone who has put the cash up but failed to run a good business, you can often save the business and the jobs with systems and processes that can save the business - and guess what, I have a whole section on this later.

TOP TIP

When starting a business, make sure you have leverage or margin. You want to make sure you have a chance of high gross profit on sales - business is much easier with high margins than tight ones.

I know you're itching to read my rules for success and how I manage this loony life and business. Wait no more you shall not, they are coming up next.

PART TWO

SUCCESS

And how to achieve it

The Rules Of Success

1.

KNOW WHO YOU ARE AND WHERE YOU'RE GOING

Your actions, your energy, your productivity, your enthusiasm are what it's all about. You just have to decide who you are, what you want and where you're going.

Hard work is a massive part of success in personal development and business, but before it can be effective, you have to decide in your head what you want.

You would be shocked just how many business owners (and people generally) don't actually decide what they want from life. They go through life just working hard from day to day, without vision or a direction. Imagine getting into a car and just driving off without thinking about your destination. Wouldn't it be a good idea to decide where you want to go before you start? This applies to business too - a million times over.

I decided very early on that I would become the busiest, and in my own heart the best, kids' entertainer in the UK – and I did it, in five years. Not only did I achieve that, I started 15 other people off in their careers - technically the 7000 parties we do a year as a company cement my achievement.

I then decided that I would create a national brand, Partyman. That decision reflects on everything we do in the business. I did not have the money to do this and I was only 19, but I had made the decision, and that gave me vision. I could then write myself a set of goals to reach my vision. With this thought cemented in my head, I was determined to make it a business. I admit that up until recently it was all about turnover, building a team, building a brand, infrastructure, systems that could roll out to the masses - it was about building something I loved.

That was what I decided, anyhow. Once you have some traction and experience, you need to understand that all that building has to be cemented by profit. That profit will strengthen what you do. I now fiercely understand that profits will strengthen my systems and give me the money to invest in building the best team and the best brand, with an infrastructure and systems that could be rolled out to the masses. 'Build build build' is a dangerous trap, so every now and then you need times of 'profit profit profit' before you return to 'build build build'. You see when you build, more often than not profit takes a hit. Knowing when to let operations lead sales is a crucial skill for SME businesses to grasp. We all want great businesses, but sometimes profits and sales keep you alive in the early days. When you have a chance you then need to use those profits to invest in operations to gain greater sales and use less of the main entrepreneur's time.

Once I had realised that profit is the key to what I call 'super-success', less stress and doing great things to make life easier, I decided it needed to be in the fabric of what I do, so much so that I have set myself a personal vision statement for myself and for Partyman. Here it is:

THE MILLIONAIRE CLOWN

To be a happy multimillionaire to allow myself to do the things that I want in life and to make things happen for my business and the people around me for greater success and happiness. I am the man who makes things happen, I think big and achieve, and above all I have a huge residual income to help me do this.

And here is my business mission statement for my Partyman brands and its family of companies. It's blasted out on posters and regularly repeated to our team. We even have it on our staff induction pack and with our full-time trainers:

We are the customer experience experts with amazing, profitable brands that families love. We believe in deadlines and making things happen. This helps us to be the best company we can be, every single day.

I believe very strongly that people need these statements. Write one down now for you and your business. I can't emphasise enough how important this is. You must have a vision of what you want. To take your company the right way - you need to know where you're going. This is not a set of goals - the goals are the map, if you like, to get you to the destination - but ultimately they define how you see yourself.

I put people or business owners into categories according to how successful they are and ultimately how they think. This then helps me to put them on a scale as to how good they are as business owners. I have three categories with varying levels in each of the three. Let's learn these little puppies so you can honestly decide which one you are. I put these into what I call the 'entrepreneur's pyramid'. The top of the pyramid is the Eagles, followed by Oxes (Oxen) and Sheep.

Eagles

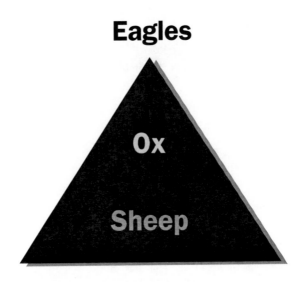

Where are you on the entrepreneurs' pyramid? Are you a Sheep, an Ox or an Eagle?

The entrepreneurs' pyramid is my key describer for business owners, leaders and to be fair, people in general. I put business owners into three categories: plodders, who I call sheep, hard workers, who I call oxes (oxen), and eagles - the business magicians who ace at running super-successful operations with a happy life. Let's meet them.

The Sheep – the plodder

These guys just work hard to get a wage, either employed by someone or in their own business. Yes that's right, many business owners own a business and only make a wage for their extra efforts over being employed. You'd be shocked just how many business owners work for a wage – they spend their lives just plodding along, always working for wages. So many business owners are stuck in a rut rather than working towards financial freedom.

Why? Because they lack vision, passion and determination to learn. Boy, do these guys love to moan! It's always someone else's problem. Sheep moan and bleat and use excuses when things aren't working. Common excuses that Sheep make for not reaching super-success are:

- *The staff aren't good enough.*
- *It's the recession/the economy.*
- *The Government's stopping us.*
- *Sorry, that's out of my comfort zone.*
- *No, we don't do that here.*
- *Sounds a bit complicated to me.*
- *Softly softly catchee monkey.*
- *What if it goes wrong?*
- *We'll wait a few years.*

In truth they can't decide what they want, so they just spin around wasting time and eating grass, day in, day out, no planning, no risk, no fire in the soul. They believe investing in themselves would be a waste of money. They would feel stupid or fail at doing anything more than the norm.

The Ox

I have a lot of affection for the Ox and it's a real passion of mine to help get this group of people to the next level of the business pyramid. Do you see yourself as a hard-working business person who turns lots of money and bulldozes through things? I was this guy, until I learned to change my approach. They implement most of the rules but forget the importance of profit, because they don't focus or invest in themselves or in systems - mainly because they spend too much time IN the business and not enough time ON it. They chase new customers and use shitty marketing that fails to impress, but they also lack a knowledge of marketing skills that really work. They think marketing is a specialist skill or a waste of money, but no, it's not - it can be learned. Oxes need to invest in themselves and become better marketers for their business to become more successful. They fail at basics, but they do achieve much more than the sheep (they probably represent 20% of the population). They are trying hard to become the next stage, which I affectionately call Eagles. The Ox is really a plodder with drive and determination added, but lacking the big picture or wide view thinking, or the vision for the future.

Let me be clear - this type of business owner or person can turn millions and have the chance to reach the next level. Usually they will, but they take decades to do it.

The number one phrase that sums these guys up and stops them going further is 'If you want a job done properly, do it yourself', an approach that lets any businessman, entrepreneur or leader down.

Common things the Ox says are:

- *I'm run ragged.*
- *I'll fit that in later.*
- *I've just got to do such and such before I can plan my month.*
- *I'll give that a try.*
- *I might read one book a year, when I'm on holiday.*
- *I work hard trying to do better.*
- *I don't have time for that meeting.*

- ■ *I don't need a PA, it's a cost.*
- ■ *I can do that myself.*
- ■ *Give that a go, it will sort my problems.*
- ■ *Cash flow's sure to get better soon.*
- ■ *That job will pay some wages.*
- ■ *That turnover will pay some wages.*
- ■ *Five years and we'll have a lovely business.*

The Ox tries hard to force his way out of his trap, but he never gives himself the chance to learn the right way to do it. He needs better time management. Just every now and then the Ox has moments of super-success, and this keeps him going, but the fear of failure holds him back.

Ultimately, I believe that until I wrote this book I was a high-end Ox myself. But through learning and taking time to be on my business I am moving into the category below...

The Eagles – the magicians

Do you see yourself as a person who makes things happen, has a great life, is never stressed out and makes lots of money - and more importantly is HAPPY? Eagles invest in themselves above all else. They never stop learning or following the rules that I've outlined in this book - they focus on profit as well as building a business, they put systems, processes and consistency at the heart of the vision and decisions they have made. If they are really awesome, they build a brand that has massive net worth at the same time.

They understand a vital rule – *LEARN and you EARN.* Luckily, you're reading this book – so you're making a step towards achieving both.

The common traits of Eagles are:

- They understand that sales and marketing are the key to business growth and profits, and they invest time in them. They know they are marketers of their business rather than workers or managers.
- They spend time ON the business, not IN it.
- They invest in holidays and take time out to reflect.
- They plan and then implement.
- They are happy.
- They are inspirational.
- They are always aware that time is short.
- They are master goal-setters and deadline-setters.
- They have a vision or a mission, which is written down – one for life, one for business.
- They have the persistence to get things done - persistence is a key factor in successful people.
- Above all they have a VISION - they have decided what they are or what they are to become.

Remember it's the RIGHT learning, not some of the tosh that's out there. Be smart and learn the right stuff – not at school, not at university, but from people out there who have actually done it. Find a mentor!

Remember, you have to DECIDE to be a millionaire or to be super successful. Many business owners never do that - they are just happy to have a business. I was never content with that. I decided I wanted to be super-successful in what I do, and I am, but I never decided I wanted to be a millionaire, so that was a fundamental problem that held me back at first. I was an Ox who decided he wanted to be successful and became an Eagle. Now, in writing this book and learning and following the rules you are about to read, I am an Eagle – a low-flying one so far, but climbing the ladder. This last point is an interesting one, because you do have low-level and high-level Oxes, Sheep and indeed Eagles, for example the Richard Bransons, Steve Jobs, Donald Trumps of this world are (were) all high-level Eagles.

Now you can be a high-level Sheep who is nearly an Ox and you can be a high-level Ox or a low-level Eagle, but honestly, knowing which one you are is critical to success - then you can invest time in moving up the entrepreneur pyramid.

TOP TIP

Decide what you are – reflect and do it now, but first write the thing down. Have a look at my example below.

I James Sinclair am a millionaire with the personal bank balance to prove it and an impressive set of assets, profits, brands and businesses to back it up. What's more I am happy, hard-working, focused and ready to be the ultimate business man, a frikin' superhero business leader!

What you are and where you come from means nothing to the success you can achieve. Just decide. I was a kids' magician-cum-clown, now I am the business magician. So do it - decide what and who you are.

Don't forget that others will see you the way you see yourself. If you come across as a hard-working guy who has built up businesses, then that's who you are. You will attract more of the same. You will by rights talk to other business owners in this bracket, and learn to love surrounding yourself by people on the next level to you, live by the phrase *If you're the smartest person in the room, then you're in the wrong room.* A later chapter will go into more detail on this.

If you decide that you're the Eagle and people believe that what you touch turns to gold (don't forget hard work is what makes things turn to gold, but it has to be the RIGHT work), think who you'll attract to your circle. Richard Branson spends time with world leaders, high-powered business tycoons and the cream of the business world. That's how he builds his wealth and network, which all help to make him the ultimate eagle. When you surround yourself with these types of people it makes your subconscious believe you *are* them!

TOP TIP

Before you work another day, decide what you are.

This is your vision, your personal mission statement. You need it, and your business needs it. Don't make the mistake of thinking you can replicate another company. Some companies will say 'I want to be the BMW of my market' or 'I want an image like Apple'. Only BMW can be BMW and only Apple can be Apple. You have to be what you are.

How you make profit and wealth for y ourself and your business

There is more than one way you can grow in wealth. You buy and sell, you create passive income (which I call residual income, the beauty of all businesses - more on this later). But the business also rises in value through its assets, profits, system and structure, achieving steady cash receipts, and it's worth a premium if it becomes a trusted, recognisable brand.

To me, the first proper way to make profit is what you get into your personal bank account or a business pays its shareholders, yet can still run on without needing that cash – otherwise it's not true profit. Do not be fooled by paper profits or what is lodged at Companies House.

The second way, and the place where super-wealth comes from, is the worth of the business. Always build a business to sell, even if you don't intend to sell it. Many of my circle of business owners tell me that if you want to be wealthy, you need to sell a business. Sadly they are right, but my main business, Partyman, is a proper business which I want to grow. You can never say never, but it's true that most super-successful business owners have sold something and made a big wedge, then started again. It gives them a cash pile and an easy life. Also, if you start again you can start with the right money to do it bigger and better and quicker, without answering to anyone.

Before we go any further, let's consider these statements and tips:

'If you want to have an easier life, always think - if you were not the owner of your business would you invest in it, or buy it?'

and

'Always build a business with the intention of selling it, even if you don't want to.'

I would rather buy a business that has systems, databases, a great brand and customers who love it, residual income, consistency and a team that has £1 million net profit as opposed to one that has one great owner-manager and £3 million net profit. Chances are the latter is the key man who is making it all happen, and without him it will flounder.

So in summary - invest in brand, team, systems, good accounts and residual income and the value is massive. Luckily this book will go into all of this!

Managing your attitude, or as I like to say your STATE.

This little nugget below really is something to take in and digest. Running or owning a business, or indeed becoming a great leader or influencer in a company and doing it well, means you need to manage your attitude, your frame of mind. You need to have what I call 'bounceability', so you can bob back up again after the bad days and deal with the problems which will always happen – that's life and that's business. We all have shitty days, it's how you deal with them and how fast you bounce back from a bad situation - that's the trick in making things happen and ultimately leading a happy life.

Your state needs to be positive - you are the expert, and experts do not flounder at every problem, they don't get stressed on every occasion. I like to say 'A calm man is a wise man', and I've found this saying very useful.

Stress and bad news are facts of life, and when you get them you need to manage them, or you won't be able to run a super-successful business. When I get down in the dumps, as everyone does every now and then, I try not to let it last for hours. I do all I can to bring myself back by reminding myself of all the positives I have achieved.

Through my years of employing thousands of people looking after millions of customers, I have discovered one important fact about people - some have happiness and bounceability for when the shit hits the fan, while others like to dwell on every bit of bad news that life serves them. Most people are somewhere in between, but successful entrepreneurs and indeed happy people (or as I call them, Eagles) have tremendous bounceability and persistence in the face of bad news.

Simply put, I have decided that to manage your attitude and be happy you simply need to make a decision – tell yourself you are going to be happy and you're halfway there. We are not looking for airheads, you need to be realistic too, but it's a massive element in getting on in life and running a business. So just have a word with yourself. In the face of adversity be happy, be positive, and then watch what happens around you – that's right, everyone else starts to look happy too. They are taking their cue from you, the one in charge. I have made a firm promise to myself - as long as I live I will maintain a positive attitude, so that I and those around me can achieve happiness in life.

Of course, I still have bad times too, sometimes - but they last for days or hours, not weeks, months or years.

TOP TIP

It's a crucial skill to know when sales need to lead operations and when operations should lead sales.

2.
WRITE DOWN YOUR GOALS

You need to know exactly how you are going to achieve your vision – but first you need to know what that vision is. Defining and writing down your goal, or set of goals, is a vital early step to success and getting the job done. And I mean, literally write them down. Trust me, it works. It's the people who say they have goals in life who always seem to be more successful. Try starting the day by writing down what you're going to get done before the sun goes down and you will achieve far more. You'll be better organised, more methodical and more focused, and you'll waste less time.

I guarantee that if you write down a list of things you really want to achieve and date them, you will make it work. In fact I suggest you draw up a to-do list for your life to meet the vision we discussed earlier, as well as one for your day. Knock all those thoughts and ideas that go through your head into shape by putting them down on paper - then you'll know what you really want to achieve.

In the early days I would use every New Year's Eve as a goal-setting day and a time to reflect on the previous year. That was the day when I would give us all a pat on the back for all the wonderful things we had done, but more importantly, I would plan ahead for the coming year. Yet I made one mistake – I never wrote those goals down. If only I had, I would be able to look back now at past years and remember what we were thinking and planning.

These days I have my goals framed and sitting on my desk, and next to each of them I write the date I want to achieve the goal by. Not all of them are business goals - some are personal and some involve self-development, which are equally vital to a successful work life. You can't just be thinking business the whole time, or it will consume you.

I believe also that it's useful to have a set of goals to be achieved over the next two months. It helps massively to make things happen in the short term. But any new goal that comes into my head that might stop the first set of goals being achieved has to go on to the next set of two-month goals – don't have too many goals, because you can't do everything at once.

I also have a set of the life goals I want to achieve by the time I'm 35. My current desk list covers the next five years, and when they're achieved and I have gone above and beyond the list I will do a new five-year set, but ultimately the goals are all set to meet my life mission and business objective, the steps to the journey I want to take. The list does need to be finished and implemented. Lots of business owners lack the stamina to make their goals happen or get disappointed if they don't reach them, or worse still disappointed when they reach them because they don't have an overall vision - they just tick off goal after goal, rather than having an overriding vision. If you're not implementing your goals, you're not building a route towards your vision.

Sometimes I may be a few months out if the goals are a little optimistic (let's be honest - sometimes I have been a whole year out!) but I always get there. It just might take a few more months than planned, even years if it's a real biggy. Keep all your goals realistic and achievable.

We all have dreams. You might say you would like a new car, a better job or a great holiday, pay off your mortgage, lose weight, write a book, get a pay rise etc, but until you commit them to paper these are all fly-by-night ideas - put them on paper and you will see them materialise. I do the same when I meet new people, to remember their names. I pretend to write the names in my pocket using my finger, then say the name three times in my head, and then it's there. With hundreds of staff, this is a massive help. The brain stores things better when you write them down.

Make sure your goals are specific. Don't write: 'I am going to be a millionaire' or 'I am going to lose weight'. Write: 'I will have one million pounds worth of assets or money in the bank on my 30th birthday, the 1st of September 2015' or 'on the 25th December 2015 I will weigh no more than 12 stone'. That way you've nailed it – and when you've achieved it, you'll know it.

After all, what IS a millionaire? A million in cash, property, antiques, bonds, shares? Your personal value, or the worth of the business? And what does losing weight mean? Does it mean cutting your waist measurement, or your weight on the scales? You must be specific in your goals.

Try these for your business:

'I have made our sales team double in size with a 30%
increase on year to date profit (enter your year-end date).

Or:

'I have increased turnover by 20% month on
month as of... (year-end date).

Then get your staff, and your departments if you have them, to write down lists of goals for their areas of business, and give rewards for hitting them. This could be simple things like, 'We got 5000 likes on Facebook - Christmas 2015' or 'We gave training to every member of staff in the year ending March 2016'.

Getting senior staff to set goals for departments and managers is a favourite of mine.

Get a one-day-per-page diary and write achievements to be completed on top of the pages, then watch the success and efficiency improve.

At the time of writing I am also putting together a five-year business plan for Partyman which sees it achieve certain goals, such as another line of residual income, turnover of £15 million and profits of £1.5 million, goals which are all set within a clear plan. I also do budgets for turnover and profit for each month. I put them behind my desk on a big board so I can scrutinise the accruals from my accounts team – that's the turnover and profit I want. It's simple and realistic and it keeps me focused on achieving these goals. The budgets form part of my plan, but I also have a business set of goals to achieve which are not financial that are essential to the business development and its future, which could include training and sales programmes or new product launches.

TOP TIP

Set short-term goals – two months

God, these work! I am a big fan of short-term goals. It's so rewarding when you see them implemented and crossed off the list. Mine go everywhere with me and when any downtime hits my desk, I pick them up and chase the world to get my goals done.

One final thing on goal setting. If you just live life by goal setting without a vision, the feeling of success and achievement will be short lived. If you think that every time you achieve a goal you need to achieve another goal, then another goal, to be happy, well you won't - you will constantly want to achieve goals to feel good. It's far better to think 'achieving this goal helps me to get closer to my vision for my life'.

The Rules Of Success

3.
OST – OBJECTIVE, STRATEGY AND TACTICS

Goal setting is a little difficult to roll out to your business, because to me, goals should be personal attributes to the individual. However, I believe the business needs to have a set of aims to get the team behind you to reach your business vision or objective, so for a business I devised a similar way that's not so personal to me - your team don't want to know if you're planning a new house in the country or trying to lose weight or aiming to learn a new language, for instance - so I created OST. Let me explain this little beauty that's so simple to implement.

Objective is the building of the ultimate vision for the business. Strategies and tactics are the business goals to meet the objective. I got into this way of thinking for my business because it's easy for the team to get involved with it. I set the objectives, they come up with the plans to achieve them. Many a successful leader has this mantra, and luckily this came naturally to me.

I call it the 20-70-10 rule. I come up with the first 20 percent of a new objective, the vision and the idea, then my team dive in and come up with 70% of the work and the detail. Then I dive in to add my last views and ideas for the last 10% to challenge the detail and add some last bits of Jimbo magic - this is simply how I can get so much done compared with most people and run a business that operates in many different sectors.

Let me explain in detail, but first ask yourself - and be honest - does your business have a clear objective? Ask a member of staff now if they know what it is. In fact, ask yourself! I didn't do this until recently when I realised this was the way to go, because your objective has to be impressed on to every one of your people.

Your objective could be set for achievement in one year, five years, 10 years or even over your whole lifetime, but you must have one. And it must stay in place until it's achieved. Then it will either remain in place or be replaced by another objective that could take you even further - for example 'We are the world class providers of X'. If you achieve the status and objective, you must then maintain it, for example.

Imagine you are fighting a war and the objective is to defeat the enemy and free the people. The strategy will be to do it over one year and the tactics might be to send an air patrol in on day one, or perhaps to enlist the help of allies to merge forces. The objective must be very simple, so the troops know why they are fighting. I am no warlord, but I believe the same is true for business- it must be that simple. Keep it Simple Stupid - KISS.

The strategy and tactics, the devil in the detail, are for the officers to work out. Strategy and tactics can change, but the objective must stay on track, and you need to share this with your people. You could even have sub-categories within the overall 'OST' plan.

For example, if you say to your team that your department has to turn over £1 million with a 15% profit margin, then that's the objective. Now let's work out a strategy and tactics for achieving it. This clearly defines how a business operates. It's also dead easy to communicate in these terms to the team. Most SMEs don't have this - they just keep on running, growing maybe 4-10% a year, because they don't actually have an objective. The boss may have it spinning around in the mind jungle, but if it's not defined, written down and communicated to the team, it's not going to be effective.

At Partyman my main business, our objective, is to very simply carry out our mission statement:

'We are to be famously known as customer experience innovators with national, profitable brands that families love. We believe in happiness, deadlines and getting things done. This helps us to be the best company we can be, every single day.'

It's simple and clear to understand. We have no worries about changing our strategies and tactics to achieve it – in fact I would say we change our strategy and tactics every 3-5 years as the business grows, through our business plan. This is our 'devil in the detail'. Even if you don't have the strategy and tactics, at least please get the objective clear.

We have a number of objectives in our mission statement, and they are all important. We clearly state we are customer experience innovators, so our team know customer service is a key objective for us. Secondly, we state that we are a national brand, so yes, everyone needs to know who we are. Then we say we are profitable, so everyone clearly knows we are here to make a profit. We then go on to mention that we believe in deadlines and getting things done in a happy way, to be the best, because that's our objective.

Objectives must be simple. I think ours could be simplified further, for example: 'The business will be the best in its sector', or 'We will be the biggest in the country'. Whatever the objective is, it comes first. I passionately believe in our objective, so it stays put.

TOP TIP

A lesson I have learned in business is this: decide very early on if you want to be a shit-hot small business that makes good money or a big business, because medium is the hardest place to be. You must know why you want to be bigger. Many businesses, like mine, double or triple turnover and make no more profit when they scale up - in some cases they make less. You may need to be 10 times bigger to see a return on your time and investment than when you were small. So decide - small making a great profit, or big.

4.

PEOPLE – FINDING THEM, WORKING WITH THEM, DEVELOPING THEM AND KEEPING THEM

Without a team that's effective, happy and fully signed up to your rules, your mission and your objectives, you are limited in what you can achieve - time runs out. So if you want super-success you need good and great people to help you do it - FACT.

Make sure your people know your mission statements, objectives and rules of work. It helps your team to focus their energies in line with yours, and more importantly, they will quickly know if they fit in with you. This is simple but breakthrough stuff. If you can get this into your head, you will have something most businesses don't. People want to know they will be led and what the journey is all about.

Most business owners never get over this hurdle. Similarly, it's your responsibility to get it into your teams. If you do this you will be, in my opinion, in the top 10% of the business owners in the country. It's so easy - and it's free. Just let people into your journey.

Why do you think some businesses are super-successful and most are not, but just get by? Is it because the owners are not very good at business or they don't work hard enough? No – it's because they lack the ability to attract great thinkers and people to join them in carrying out the objective.

To be effective, teams need to understand the journey they are on. I am a big believer that people will love you for letting them know where you are going, and where you are taking them. They can then decide whether or not to give you more than just their time for your money. Remind them of the journey they're on, remind them of your mission statements and your objectives.

People who work for us very quickly realise that we have standards and that we passionately believe in the customer experience which keeps our customers coming back. We believe in profit and we don't muck about, but also we put a big emphasis on being the best, every day.

When your staff understand your company mission and their leader's vision, you will automatically hold yourself and your team accountable for the actions you are taking.

I also think it's important to have a set of rules that fit the work ethics you wish for. Here are my head office rules:

1. We employ only happy, hard-working people who are on brand for our business. Those who are not must believe or leave.

2. We train our people well enough so that they get offers to leave, but treat them well enough that they want to stay.

3. We work a hard, full day.

4. We are a team - saying 'that's not my job' is the same as saying 'sack me now'.

5. We do things quickly. We follow deadlines. We achieve or we leave.

6. We are here to make a profit.

7. We don't waste money.

8. We never, ever, waste time.

9. We keep our uniforms and workwear tidy and our desks and offices tidy – we declutter at all costs.

10. We don't clock-watch. If we have to work a little later or through the night to reach a deadline, then so be it. We do this because we believe in what we are doing.

11. Believe or leave – it's simple.

12. We set deadlines and finish stuff.

13. We have goals set to achieve success at work.

14. We speak up and offer great ideas, and mention stuff we don't like or think we can do better.

15. We are all mini-marketers doing all we can to promote our lifetime objective of becoming customer experience innovators with a national profitable brand that families love.

16. If there's a choice between the customer's favour and the company's favour, then if it's marginal we will support the customer.

17. YES is the word - not nasty NO.

Of my customer-facing people, I ask only one thing - follow the four Es in everything you do at work:

- Enthusiasm
- Engagement
- Entertainment
- Equalling an Experience

What does that really mean, an experience? to me an experience is what I believe people now crave and want, and they will pay for it. A good experience or an outstanding experience means you don't become the 'me too business'. What I mean by that is that you become the company that competes on experience and not on generalist services and, more importantly, price.

People are the lifeblood of a business and the best way to help push the emphasis of the experience you wish to create. Yes, there are business owners who say 'bloody staff!', or 'If you want a job done, do it yourself' or 'You can't have good staff, otherwise they would be doing it themselves'. If that's how you think, you're a useless leader who does not get the basics – simple!

Now don't get me wrong - I have been victim to many staff problems and no one is perfect. I am the first to admit that I couldn't work for anyone - I would get sacked on day one. I am far too set in my ways and far too opinionated, and I get frustrated if something's not good enough. Good and great staff are there, and I have some fantastic people, but just like great families, they need time and love - and a cuddle every now and then.

If you really make it in business and leadership - and it takes time, effort and planning - you will realise that it needs a lot of thought and implementation, but to really get to 'eureka' you need your senior team to do the same. They need to become great thinkers and implementers of the strategies and tactics to deliver your objectives. Get it right and they will mimic you and become mini-entrepreneurs themselves within your business. Get a couple of these bad boys working for you and watch your company transform!

Your team

The people, the team, the staff - call them what you will, they are your greatest asset and they can accelerate growth or alternatively destroy you. Why are they your greatest asset? Because they give you time to work on building the business. I still say that the marketing of the business is the essential asset, because if no one knows about you, you get no sales, so you must build a team you are proud of.

Eventually, as you grow, you may need dozens, hundreds, even thousands of staff. Looking after them needs care, time and attention to detail, and further time will be needed to spread the ethos of your company. I have been to many seminars where I've heard business owners talk about this. I have also spoken to many employees of other firms, and it shocks me how many people get the basics wrong.

It's all about who you take on at interview (and we do still make mistakes – you're not alone, but we get better at this all the time). You need to be fussy and recruit on hard work, ethics and personality, not what a CV says. You will be shocked how many people don't even write their own CVs. When I interview people I make a point of saying at the start of the interview that I have not read their CV and won't look at it until later in the interview - sometimes not at all - and when I do so I just look to make sure they haven't had 10 jobs in two years, as I want people who can stick things out, not those who have worked here for a year, there for a year etc.

The smaller you are, the easier it is to create a great team. When I had three staff we were the most highly motivated, well-organised, well-oiled machine you would ever find. The staff were loyal, the relationship was strong and we never missed a trick. Looking back, it was because I invested time in teaching them the way I wanted things done. They loved it, because they had a direct link to me. Now we need to work on systems and processes to make that still happen. As our business gets bigger this is becoming easier in some ways, yet at the same time more challenging.

In effect the old-school way of you getting paid to do a job works fine, but make sure this is not littered with stupid, petty rules. Use rules that make a difference. Rules need to be for the greater good, not a mishmash of systems that don't work. The rules I set out at the start of the chapter are for my head office team, and they are very different from the front-of-house rules for a service industry and a chain of day nurseries which we also own. I am working hard with the heads of these departments to make a set that fits for them, but the ethos is still exactly the same.

A great friend and mentor of mine, Andrew Wolfe, runs a farming and leisure business, as well as being a super-businessman with all the right ethics and leading a super motivated team. Andrew says: 'people earn a wage to give you their hands for the time they are working for you, but if you're doing a really good job of looking after them they will give you their hearts, and this is when the business will go from strength to strength.'

Mentors and friends like Andrew are true diamonds. The Andrews of the world are out there and they need to be kept close, because learning from great people helps make you great. When you come across them in life, hold on to them. As I write I just want to thank Andrew for all his words and wisdom over the few years we have known each other - I bloody love the man, as well as his wife Anna.

Sure, it's a little more complicated than this, and nowadays more than ever at Partyman we are fussier about the people we employ - we recruit on personality and hard work first. I always say to our team, are they on brand? Do they fit the company's personality? That word 'brand' is always the topic of conversation and when I say 'on brand' I mean are they on trust, trust that they will deliver the brand values we promise our customers? Never forget - the word 'brand' means trust.

Qualifications and experience should always come second to personality. You always want to try to employ happy, hard-working people for any business. Happy people are the people who make other people flourish and encourage prospects, customers and other businesses, or guests as we call them, to interact with you and do business with your company.

Remember that not always paying the most money gets you the best team. I have met lots of people on high salaries who wouldn't last a week under us. Some 16-year-olds we have employed fresh out of school have wiped the floor with some experienced adults, because they are happy and hard-working.

Ethos, mission statement and simple objectives will get you to where you want to be fast. I am also a big believer that as you grow you should recruit a 'super trainer' to work in house and train, train and train again. your team will love it - you learn about problems and create great communication. We have a new department called 'Magic Makers' which just trains, nurtures and cuddles our people with practical training, not stupid lengthy corporate bullshit that doesn't help anyone – It has to be fun, whatever business you're in.

Know this - training once a year or every 3-6 months, or even worse, a day's shadowing on your first day, is no good for the business or the team. It has to be consistent, consistent and even more consistent. And if you take over a business, something I have often done, and the people don't embrace the training and development, refer them back to the rules – namely, believe in what we are trying to do here or leave! Time is short, very short.

Disney are so good at this. They even send staff to Disney University for two weeks before they start in any role. That's why to this day people will pay a premium for Disney products and services, simply because people will pay for great experiences led by Disney employees. They never have to compete on price. They one hundred percent compete on experience, and they are probably the world market leader in customer service and experience.

As I said earlier, we tell our customer experience team to follow the four Es in our business, to give them the tools to work for a great brand they respect and love just as much as me – Engagement, Enthusiasm, Entertainment and Experience.

Putting simple values up around the workplace and implementing them with starter packs, training and continually asking your people for ideas on how we can improve the above will hit home, telling your team what you want from them and what they have to do to be part of it.

I know my business happens to be based on leisure, education and entertainment, but core values work whatever your business is. For example, for my nurseries it's:

Engagement

Education

Enthusiasm

= a great childcare experience

For lawyers it could be:

Expertise in our knowledge and our advice

Enthusiasm in our work and to help our clients

Engagement to our colleagues and clients

= a great legal experience

What does your business have as its set of four Es, or set of values?

We also fill our contracts with fun stuff that staff will read before they start working for us. Thought, love and care have been put into this so that our people know who we are and what we want them to be.

When we recruit customer experience staff (remember experience is the new word for service) we put them up on stage and tell them to talk about their personality and life. All the other interviewees then form the audience and watch.

Remember: staff who want to work hard need investment in them to develop, just as you should as a leader - a know-it-all knows nothing!

People want to work with leaders, not for bosses, so be a leader, not a boss. Leaders are approachable - so should you be.

OK, we don't recruit our accounts or admin staff like this, but we still find out if they are happy, hard-working and reliable first. We have no room for moody people – happy, hard-working people only need apply!

Be a LEADER – not just a boss

Leadership is essential to creating a successful business, and great leaders manage to make leaders too.

While leadership is something that comes naturally to some, I firmly believe that those to whom it isn't second nature can also learn to lead effectively - you may be a little rough around the edges at first, but that doesn't mean you can't become truly great, given experience, mentorship and learning.

Becoming a good leader means understanding and accepting that not everyone thinks like you. More importantly, the people you are leading have to know what you want to achieve. You have a passionate vision of what you want for your enterprise, whether it's a business, a charity, a political organisation or anything else, and it's this vision that gives your people a reason to follow you.

It shocks me just how many people are expected to do a job without a reason or a vision – and if the leader doesn't have one, how can the ones who are supposed to follow the leader have one?

Leaders need to be perceived as experts through skills, experience, charisma and influence - and if they want to succeed they need to have the ability to be ON the team, not just IN the team.

Let's look at some types of leader I've encountered.

Short-term leaders

Short-term leaders are effective at making change happen quickly.

They shock the team into ideology and carry them along on a tidal wave – but tidal waves don't last, and they can leave a lot of damage behind them. Look at Adolf Hitler!

I have met plenty of short-term leaders who lose traction because they go off vision, and people no longer believe in them or want to fight for their cause. People often start jobs for new companies attracted to the vision and a burning desire to be part of it - trouble is, it doesn't come to fruition, and these short-term leaders who have the ideas but lack the get up and go soon flounder, as does the team around them.

Long-term leaders

This is what business leaders should aspire to be, consistent good leaders – think of great entrepreneurs like Sir Richard Branson and Steve Jobs. You want your people to be led by you and stick by you for the long term – plenty of our best leaders are still firmly in charge long after the normal retirement age.

Entrepreneurs need to become great leaders if they want to be super successful, and I do believe that leaders in this category are very different from leader managers. Businesses and organisations need both kinds, yet it's very rare to encounter entrepreneurs who can do both well. You need leaders with vision, but you also need people to keep an eye on the detail.

The entrepreneur or vision leader, for example the head teacher of a school, needs to make sure the team are buying into his or her vision, so they know why they are doing it, and they know the journey they are on.

Think about how this works in the film industry. You have producers with the vision to raise the money, recognise a great story or script and make it all happen, but then a director harnesses the producer's vision by bringing the film to the screen. The Indiana Jones series was one of the most successful in box office history. George Lucas, the producer, was the long-term visionary leader there, while Steven Spielberg was the director - the leader-manager.

Leader-managers

Businesses and organisations need managing as well as leading. Bosses who lead the people they look after know the difference between professional leadership and not becoming everyone's friend. Ultimately people want to be led by people they respect as leaders, and this professional relationship must not be compromised by favouritism or unduly close friendships. I see this so much with managers who single out favourites – it damages their ability to manage well, and even if they are careful to apply the same standards to everybody, those who feel they are not part of the boss's 'clique' will imagine they are being treated differently, which can build resentment. So by all means socialise with the team, go out with the team, reward the team, but never choose favourites among them. Reward top achievers - but demonstrate that the same rewards are available to all, and ensure they all know how to achieve them.

Good leader-managers handle strategies and tactics exceptionally well and are champions of devil-in-the-detail stuff, but like Superman drawing his power from the sun they still need to harness power from a motive, a reason for why they are doing it. They manage the vision. If you want a successful organisation or business you need leader-managers, as I call them, in all core areas.

Leader-managers want to work with entrepreneurs who have vision and leadership too - they are usually super-motivated and help to drive the machine.

NOTE: Entrepreneurs – typically CEOs, owners, chairmen and/or founders - can and should become great friends with their managing directors. They should think alike and answer alike and become super trustworthy of each other, though different. They are the yin and yang of the business and respect each other entirely. To make a child grow you need a mum and a dad, and in my opinion business or organisational success needs an entrepreneur and an MD.

Bad leaders - 'bosses'

We all know them, we have all met them - the old-fashioned bosses who have black and white rules and lay down what's right and what's wrong. With no flexibility In my business with the exception of certain key issues mentioned above – mainly about staff commitment to the company and its mission, which is not optional - people who work directly for me have always had as much freedom as they want. Naturally this doesn't work for all businesses - certainly not service businesses - but if it's possible to give people the chance to control their own diaries, flexitime and work patterns you will be shocked how much better people with a strong work ethic prosper in these situations. This one move could catapult you from boss to leader/mentor status.

Now this does not work if you have a customer-led service business, as most of my businesses do. You can't have your kitchen staff having days off and coming in late - the whole thing would fall apart. But if people can work from home and have a lie in when they like, as long as they are responsible, people will LOVE your company. All my key team that are not needed in service can manage their work life as they see fit - as long as the job gets done. If people want to get off early to see their kids' play or say simple things like 'I have the trots, I'll work from home today', that's fine.

We all remember the best teachers at school - they stay with you forever. That's very much what a leader should be, not simply someone who dishes an appraisal out once a year. I hate that approach to appraisals - don't get me wrong, they are a useful part of managing staff if used correctly, but I firmly believe that discussing something once a year is bollocks. You should be giving praise and criticism in real time, when it's needed, every day if necessary – and that applies to both employers and employees.

Bad bosses think of staff relationships as legal agreements - think communication instead and see how much better you can be. When you get it wrong or someone has a better idea, go with it. I am a big believer in letting people try stuff that I know won't work. People will love the opportunity you gave them, just don't let it bring the whole house down - manage the risk!

Leaders are mentors who empower and create prosperity with opportunity. Good leaders continue to learn to be better. They remember in bad situations that a calm man is a wise man. Bad bosses think their way is always right. They have strict professional relationships, with no grey areas. They have favourite employees – the perfect way to p*** off everyone else!

One final thing I have found in my career is that bad leaders have a knack for retaining bad people in the business. Simply put, if you have people are wrong for the business, then they are wrong for the business.

TOP TIP

If you can't change the people, change the people.

5.
THINK BIG, ACT SMALL - EVEN WHEN YOU'RE BIG

The title of this chapter needs explaining. It's a strange piece of advice, but one that will ground you for business success.

A business that thinks big but acts small will be entrepreneurial and not littered with stupid rules and costs. It will act fast because it has an eye on the prize, but can nip it in the bud as a small business can. It will move like a tiger, not a herd of elephants.

I have to admit, looking back, the smaller we were, the more fun it all was. We were more entrepreneurial and had more laughs. I have to try very hard to keep us running like a small business, not scripted to a set of stupid rules or led by a faceless board, so I have just enough to keep us on my vision statement and the mission statement that puts us where we want to be as a company.

We also made more profit per pound back then – we just didn't have so many pounds. In fact if you go back to my first chapter, I said that you have to decide who you are. I was a little mini-magician at business, learning to be an eagle, and boy did I know how to make money out of what I had. When you get bigger, you can't run the company the same way, but you should never forget what you had. Your business will need to grow up, but try and remember the small things that got you to be a big business. Never think to yourself: *We're getting to be a big company now. Big companies have flash offices and fleets of cars, don't they? Then that's what we'll do.*

Keep your company looking and feeling small, in every way you can. Customers love it. Give a personal service - they love that too. They want to know you will care for them and deliver for them. So please try to hang on to the things that made your business work so well when you were starting up. History is littered with businesses that lost their way.

In the early days we were ridiculously profitable, because we hadn't yet reached the stage where we had to worry about those lurking burdens such as VAT, health and safety, business rates, insurance and so on. We didn't have to lash out on purpose-made furniture and office equipment (we don't do that now either, I still love a bargain), or rent dedicated business premises (we don't do that). Instead at Partyman HQ, we work out of a 400-year-old farmhouse and manage low rents and overhead for our sites. Back then, we could also manage without paying staff who were not bringing in money themselves. Inevitably your business model will change as you get bigger, with accountants, book-keepers, technical people and so on – the point is, you shouldn't let it spoil your fun. Keep an eye on those expenses that will creep into your business and try for as long as possible to let your sales lead the operations - this is the cunning advantage of a small business over a large one.

Starting small and growing bigger taught me the basics. I would run a paper tally of income and outgoings to keep myself on track and make myself feel good. It was very simple – start with a gross income for the month of say £500, then take off the cost of fuel and the net profit is say £325. As I have grown and formed companies, that £325 in every £500 has inevitably fallen to more like £100, and as it's got bigger some years we may only keep two or three per cent back.

In our sector we aim for a 10-20% margin. I'm happy to take a drop in profit when I'm building a business, but only because I'm thinking of the long term. It's planned, because I know the turnover figure has gone up many times over. You just have to remember that as the turnover grows you need to be keeping an eye on profit too, and if it's taking a nosedive whilst you grow, which usually happens, you need to plan and know what you are doing and why you are doing it. You need to know you are planning for a turnaround in the near future and that despite the short-term loss in profit, or indeed loss, the rewards will be massive when you get to the other side.

When I took Aaron on, along with some part-time admin help, I had to learn how to budget for wages every month. This meant that as a small business owner I had to wear a lot of different hats. I was the chairman and managing director, the operational manager, the finance director and the human resources director, all rolled into one. And all the time I knew I could not afford to let go of my original role - the entrepreneur who was always thinking and looking at the big picture to see how the business could flourish by moving in new directions.

You will find many people become business owners by accident, through getting laid off, through a management buy-out or a redundancy cheque which they use to invest in a start-up. These people often walk away with a nice lump of cash, then promptly blow it because, as employees of a big company, they have always been protected from the real deal of running a business. Many start a business with no idea what they are doing and lose the lot very quickly – 20 per cent of businesses fail within a year and 50 per cent within five years. Their founders may be great at the job they've been doing while working for a company – they just don't know how to apply that knowledge to making money in their own right. They have to think small but act big, instead of thinking big and acting small. Seize opportunities and let your business have a personality – that's the way to go.

Keeping it small in as many ways as possible is a great grounding for sustainability. To this day I still regularly check all our invoices and sign each one off. If there is something that has created waste or looks too expensive, I can manage it to create extra profit. When you grow, other people control the purse strings. They are happy to spend money because it's not theirs, and controlling this is a must. It's essential that suppliers and staff know that you are hot on this stuff, because people will take the mickey!

We still get three quotes for all work we do when using outside companies, even if we know and love the supplier. Keeping an eye on cash keeps you grounded. Sometimes it's a ball-ache to go through 500 invoices, but the hour it takes is essential for my business. This is small business mentality, and a skill you should stick with even when you get big.

I'll tell you another thing I do that keeps us feeling small and acting small - I still regularly work front of house, managing our peak times, answering phones to customers. I am still entertaining at our venues and doing parties at people's houses - I admit not as regularly, but still weekly. How else would I know the trends if our tills, phones and computers work well enough, or if systems are not working?

When you get big, things creep in that can sabotage your business, but small businesses never let this happen because they can't afford to - and nor should you when you get bigger.

When you grow, you must never let your business act so big that people, staff and customers are scared of you, or feel the personal touch has left you.

You and your team need to know that it's OK to make mistakes, as long as you learn by them (we still make mistakes at Partyman and

I'm not afraid to admit it – if you are not making mistakes you are probably playing it too safe and avoiding change). Be brave and tell your team - you decide! Even if you know they are making the wrong decision, it's an important learning opportunity (as long as it's not a business-critical matter). Chat it through and become the wise Yoda figure who guides and advises – not the authority figure who punishes and criticises. We need to have eight meetings with six consultants to change the colour of our logo? Dig me a grave now!

For the last year I have been working with a local government body as a consultant on a leisure business we have taken over. Any wise human or person with an ounce of business savvy will say that councils should not run businesses, and they're absolutely right. But this one *was* running a business, and it needed help.

Government bodies and big organisations like charities are so big that employees are scared of taking risks. For this reason decisions often take months to be made. Procedure, protection and policy stall their thinking. This ethos can spread very quickly in your own team as you get bigger. You may all too easily become unapproachable to your staff, because they are scared of going against the system. To you, you're just really busy – to them, it's 'don't disturb the boss', unless you want a bollocking.

Spending money is easy and it's what too many big businesses do - worse, they spend money on the wrong things. If you have spare cash, invest it in implementation for more profits, not fancy offices, private cars and frills. As soon as people start telling you that you need a human resources department, a full-time receptionist, a PR consultancy on a retainer, or a firm to look after the flowers in reception – ask yourself what life was like when you did the hiring and firing, Jenny looked after the phones, Billy popped out to get the sandwiches for lunch and you did your own PR – chances are it was a lot better. You may need all these things in due course as you get bigger (PR can raise your profits if it's done right and flowers are a nice touch once you've reached the stage of managing the experience of visiting you), but think very hard first.

Keep it small. Know when you need the things you need and when you don't Keep it tight, entrepreneurial and lean.

Costs are bad, but investments are good

Avoid costs – think only of investments in systems and procedures. What's the likely return from the money you're being asked to spend? You need to treat every pound as if it's your last, and ask if it will generate more.

Can the person who happens to be working in reception also do your book-keeping or deal with sales enquiries? in the early days these little things really work. Never lose the focus of letting sales lead operations. Do they have the skills and experience perhaps to interview new staff, or put out a press release? Use the talents you have before going out to pay for new people - I love to use 'multi skilled' in a job description.

Question every cost as if it's the last pound you have. Keep it lean and mean. Treat your business's finances as if you're going to go bust tomorrow. Too many businesses live for the day. On the other hand, don't become so cost-focused that you have to spend twice, or lose out on value. And don't become so cost-focused that you save a wage rather than build a business. It's a balance that needs a plan.

When I was 21 I turned my first million, and I thought that meant I was a millionaire. Whata div I was! I went out and bought a Range Rover, then six months later I set up a limo company. I thought I was the man - silly plonker. A stretch limo at 21? What was I thinking? I bought it without figuring out how I was going to make it work for me. As a result I managed to hire it out just 10 times.

THE MILLIONAIRE CLOWN

I used to think turning small amounts of money into big ones was as easy as one-two-three. Just setting up one business and moving on to another was a little foolish - I didn't have the mindset to do that. But I have learned from these mistakes. I had become a little too easy come, easy go. In 2007 you could get hold of nasty high-rate loans rather too easily, and I was borrowing more than I could afford in my rush to make my business grow as fast as possible.

The businesses that remember to think small are the ones you have to watch, if they are your competition. They are usually high-profile, entrepreneur-owned companies. Look at the Facebook story. It's basically a small, thinking business and from what I have read about them they have tried to keep it that way.

I had a conversation with an ex-member of staff only this week who has gone to work for someone else, a bigger company than us. A week before her birthday, she asked if she could leave work early that day - they said no. The next day, they asked her if she would take a shorter lunch because they were busy - she said no right back. It works both ways.

I hope the days are passing when big companies have named parking spaces (always nearest to the front door) and huge, plush offices for the directors, let alone separate washrooms. Not only is it a stupid waste of money, it perpetuates the 'them and us' attitude. Currently I am sharing a small office with four staff and I love the communication we have. You do need your own space to concentrate at times, and perhaps for confidential discussions, but that doesn't mean you should spend most of your working time shut away from your team.

Here's what a good leader does, in my view, to keep on thinking big but keep the entrepreneurial 'small and friendly' feeling – and you can do it yourself, however big you get.

- Make sure you're accessible, so that staff can see you and talk to you without making an appointment. Give your email and mobile out - people are not silly, they won't take your time unless they need to.

- Spare a few moments a day to chat to them about their lives as well as the work agenda. If Susie's grandmother has died and Mike's son has got a place at university, make sure you're not the last to know.

- Go and walk about the business – don't be desk driven! Do this, and do it well.

- Learn from your team– ask their advice at every opportunity. They'll love it, and love you.

- Share the same car park, washroom, kitchen etc – you're not royalty.

- Allow your staff to have a home life. If you find out it's Daisy's wedding anniversary or Jim's little brother is in the school play, invite them to take an hour or two off. They will reward you by working harder when they're in.

- Always listen to people, customers and staff - they will keep you grounded.

- As you grow, beware of recruiting new middle managers to come between you and staff you used to manage yourself. Your staff should always feel they have the ear of the leader – particularly if it's what they're used to.

- The same applies to customers. Nothing will irritate a valued customer more than being told, in effect, that the boss is now too important to look after their account. The classic saying is true - if you don't look after your customers, someone else will.

- Never forget - you're there to set an example. Look smart, but not flash. Talk smart, but don't boast or pontificate. You want to be an amazing parent, the best teacher. Keep control, stay wise and calm.

- Start early and work hard, but don't try and set an unrealistic example - make it clear you have a home life too, just as they do.

- Be informal and approachable, but don't try to make them like you by competing with them on funny stories or your knowledge of sport or pop culture (remember Ricky Gervais in The Office?) You need your staff to respect you, because however big or small your company, you are the leader who makes things happen, the person who will move mountains.

Tell your staff how you self-develop. Learn and share your goals - a developing learning team is a great team.

TOP TIP

A calm man is a wise man.

TOP TIP

Do yourself a favour, sign off invoices and work on the floor every now and then, not forever because you have a business to build, but just enough to see the sabotage off and keep your business a lean, mean machine.

6.

LEARN HOW TO RAISE FINANCE

In 2010/11 I was seeking finance to move our business forward and build a nursery in our Basildon branch with a new laser arena to create second and third revenue streams. The common thing for me to do in our business is create or bring in multiple revenue streams, and I needed some cash to do this, but the banks just didn't want to know. We had weak accounts because we were growing and using all our cash for the business, but I knew what we needed to do. I knew that without the cash to build these additional revenue streams I would never be able to progress the business, so I sought investment elsewhere. It was difficult at that time, bloody hard work, but I had a few options and met some multi-millionaires who wanted to invest in us.

My choice of investment was with a man so similar to my outlook on life it was uncanny, except that there was 40 years between us. Not only is he a man with proper wealth, but he is a lovely, down-to-earth guy and above all a genuine entrepreneur, who does the thing he does for fun and love first and then money - that's why he's so good. He cares about others, never doing anyone over, but at the same time he doesn't suffer fools gladly. As with me, the property bug is his choice for investing surplus cash, although he also has a love for old cars, the older the better. Enter my surrogate family - the Barton-Wrights.

Philip and Alice Barton-Wright are like family to me. They are just the way I want to be. They are a close family who are devoted to their children, and sometimes I wish my family was like theirs - they are just so close, and that's why they have everything.

Philip has become another mentor to me on many levels (more on mentorship later). I met him because I had a network through knowing other people. I can't emphasise enough what the power of a network can do you for you.

I get on so well with them and I'd do anything I could for them. I still say what I think, when I think and how I think. Although it's a serious investment which I know I have to pay back, knowing them and being around Philip has made me a better person, not just for business but for what is important in life. It has also taught me how to accept that you need outside help if you wish to grow and your business needs capital, and the right deal can accelerate growth.

Some businesses, such as insurance brokers, office-based and service industries, don't need cash, but my business, like all leisure sector businesses, needs big injections of money to grow - £250,000 here, £500,000 there. In the last year we have spent close to £2 million on property acquisitions, growth, business expansion and refinance. Could I have achieved this alone at 26? No, I needed security to get bank support, so I had to sell some shares to create equity and obtain security.

I wish more than anything that I had £5 million worth of unencumbered property to do it alone and borrow against. I don't, although I hope I soon will, and as Philip has done for me at 65 I intend to do for others in my older years and get them on the right path to greater success. It's quite simple - the more entrepreneurs this country produces, the better off everyone will be.

After 10 years my company now employs 300 staff and pumps millions every year into the tax system through rates, PAYE, VAT, corporation tax, insurance premium tax, fuel duty, National Insurance and all the others I have missed.

Entrepreneurs are essential for the economy. They should have freer access to cash to grow their businesses even further. We know what we are doing - we shouldn't have to sell shares if we don't want to, or get venture capitalists involved. Many have had businesses ruined by these guys, but then the Facebooks and Twitters of this world have blossomed.

Banks have always done well out of lending to SMEs in the UK. They took big risks in dodgy offshore mortgage lending- remind them of that if you get turned down for a loan.

Banks in the UK made and have made billions lending to small businesses. Collectively we are safe, and once a business has a few years' experience under its belt they should lend more freely, rather than bond markets and the like.

OK, rant over. As I write I have taken over a children's farm park in Essex, and it is now my home. It is 50 acres of magical fun, and I live right in the middle. We have super animals, tearooms and fun activities for the whole family. I bought the business from the local authority as referred to earlier, who were losing a quarter of a million quid a year. Sorting it out was right up my street. My team are well trained at business turnaround and we are doing the same here - strict cost controls, great customer service, the right offering and marketing will soon make this a magical place, oh and a little extra cash to create all the wonderful things we want to do.

So I need cash - how do I raise it?

Now I get fed up listening to successful entrepreneurs and billionaires say you don't need money to start a business. In some cases this is true. If you want to be an accountant or an insurance broker, an entertainment agency, telesales company etc, then yes they are right, hard graft will get you where you need to be and the cash will eventually come in for you to do things. Remember that - cash is just a resource to allow you to do things and keep the business going. I like enough in the bank to have easy cash flow, but easy cash flow takes years to build. It's taken me 10 years to get out of overdraft and cash positive.

But what if you are like me and your business is building stuff? Farm parks, laser arenas, day nurseries, event equipment hire, an online party shop, all need money to expand and grow. Maybe you have made a successful start and want to replicate it all next year on a different site. Some won't have the willpower to do this, but if you do you will need access to cash. Just think Costa, Facebook, Ikea. They were not everyday UK brands 10 years ago, so how did they become globally recognised like McDonalds and Tesco with only a decade's trade behind them compared to the latter with 50-plus years? They get investors, bank cash or private funds so they can accelerate the business to grow faster than it should organically. Your business, if you know what you're doing, should grow year on year organically, but a serial entrepreneur like me has the 'want it done yesterday' bug. Making money is not the goal. Building success is, and the money just happens because you build the success.

So how can you get the money? You may be lucky enough to have a million stashed away - in that case use it, but if not you have to do it the hard way, which is the way most business people have to go. The better you get, the easier it is to grow and get cash. By then of course, you don't need it as you did in the beginning.

Now before I go any further, don't think I am about to say this is how you do it, because to this day, I speak on a weekly basis to millionaires and businessmen who are far more experienced than I am, and what do they all say? Getting cash is difficult, and usually it's a long process. A multi-millionaire has just told me that it has taken five months for a loan to come through, and believe you me, he can pay it back with his eyes closed.

An option to consider, though not a way I like, is to borrow from friends or family. It's cheap, but it will put a great deal of pressure on you. I have borrowed from people I know, but only on a very short-term basis when I know I have funds coming in from the bank to replace the loan. This is not something I have entertained in recent years.

The next and cheapest way is to borrow money from the bank, although this takes time and you need to have security to get your hands on it. At the time of writing banks are simply not as liquid as they used to be since the crisis of 2008, and don't let them fool you with this 'We are willing to lend' stuff they promote in their advertising and marketing. Yes they will lend, but you have to tick a lot of boxes first. Even a class history, security and the ability to pay are brought up against difficulties.

Something that will help massively with bank finance is property, property that has little borrowing against it and preferably none. Many businesses and entrepreneurs, whether small companies or huge multinationals, have difficult times, as do all businesses at some point, but they always fare better when they have assets. Look at Marks & Spencer, struggling to keep up to date with the changing world. They took a knock on sales for a few years and needed to reinvest without delay, but did they really have to worry about cash? No way! Just go on line and look at the property they own. Exxon, when they had to pay hundreds of millions out following the *Exxon Valdez* oil spill tragedy off the coast of Alaska, managed just fine because of their holdings. An asset book of property and stocks will always see the difficult times become a lot easier, as it will for the individual entrepreneur.

Starting a business from scratch that won't make any money till year 4? This can happen. But it's OK if you have a few million in property till you get there. Watch the bank relax. They won't be happy, but they will be more comfortable.

That's why it's essential in my view to build up assets that you can use to borrow against in the future. It takes years, but you have to start somewhere. It also provides excellent pension planning. (More on property later, in its own chapter.)

Property is what banks love to lend against. It gives them security, but on the other hand, if you want to buy property or build property even if you have cash to invest as well - good luck.

Many banks will say they don't or won't be lending for investment property or property development - work that one out! Yes that's right, the very thing they want to lend against is the thing they don't want to lend for. You need to get to know the different banks and their quirky individual ways, and they do vary from bank to bank. It's essential to shop around to know the markets and get the best deal. It's essential to watch the interest rate too, because if the interest is too high it will affect cash flow in the monthly payments.

I took my first dip into using property to leverage against the business when I was 19 years old and starting the Partyman Company. I used property in business to get hold of a £150k bank loan to build the first venue I opened. I had to use £50k as a security deposit with the landlord to get access to the property in case we went belly up – you see, property does help, without that I wouldn't have got the venue.

So how did I get the £350,000 I needed to finish the job? Well, I had some of the business's cash and my own meagre savings, and I cleared both of those out - I had zilch by the time we opened. I leased all the rest, in fact I had around 15 different lenders for it – nightmare! It killed me from a cashflow point of view, it felt as if I was working for the lease companies. At my peak I had loan or lease repayments from the first month of trading of £15,000 a month - when you are starting from scratch it's a big commitment. I just wish I'd had a better understanding of all this stuff then.

Leasing companies will argue that it's quick money and they don't need property security, and boy is this right. I got money as easy as making a phone call, although this was 2006/7, but they only lend against tangible assets that can be taken away if you default. Shop around - you need to get the best interest rates, but they do lend a lot more readily than the banks and over shorter terms - 2, 3 or 5 years. The stranger the asset the higher the rate, and you need to learn the difference between interest deals. They will give you a headline figure and tell you it's tax efficient because you can claim the money back, ie its fully tax deductible, but you still have to find the repayments every month!

Without getting too complicated, in a set of accounts the bank repayments of a loan will not show up in the profit and loss (the management accounts things we spoke about earlier) but the interest part does. The capital part of your expenditure gets written off over the period of its life in depreciation, which does show in the profit and loss. All these things you have to learn, to understand why you need cash and how to use it to grow.

The actual rate of leasing equipment could be 35% APR, compared to a bank at 5%, and this will really hurt the management accounts. When I look at a business to take over, or at my own, the management accounts are far more helpful than a set of annual accounts. The problem with annual accounts is that they are done for Companies House, the bank and that lovely shareholder we all have to split our money with, the taxman. As I said before, the management accounts or profit and loss figures will help you - my bank managers have even lent money on the strength of our management accounts. What you are sending up to your bank manager will give you the edge and make it easier to borrow. With the help of my accountant I got a loan finance package worth £1.5 million when we were making a loss! I got this because I said I knew I was going to make a loss for another year. I had projections and accounts to back my argument up, so I got my grubby hands on the money I needed for the business to grow. Now we are paying it back and doing quite nicely, thank you very much.

If you have the track record of a great manager or employee, or you own a small business and want to go on to the next level and the bank just doesn't want to know, you might have to entertain the VC (venture capitalist) route. These guys will have access to big cash in the markets. It can go two ways, either to the height of all heights in terms of success or horribly wrong, and of course they take control of your business.

When going down the VC route, as long as you say what you are doing you should have a great relationship with your new partners. They will take a slice of the business for the cash they put in, and they will want the structure of a huge company, board meetings, chairmen and a huge scale-up, and at least 20% profit or returns on the cash they stump up. That's not my cup of tea. I like to keep cash tight so I can control the action. I have been lucky enough to take over a business where the VC pulled out and left the business up for grabs.

So what did I do to raise cash that the bank would not lend me? I went and got myself an experienced investor and sold some shares to him. He would let me run the business and grow it the way I wanted to, without wasting money. This allowed me to carry on being an entrepreneur. I made sure I had the option of paying him back one day. Then I had an option to borrow more from the bank because my investing partner had millions of unencumbered assets, which gave us the security to borrow to build the business. It also gave us a lump of cash to buy the freehold on one of our sites and invest in the business. Lots of growing businesses like mine are good but lack the right funding – in professional terms this is called being underfunded.

Such businesses are using the cash they are earning to grow the business rather than running it. This is where cash flow problems happen. You should always use new cash for expansion and growth, unless you have so much of your own money stored in the bank that you can afford it.

But if you're like me and a lot of serious entrepreneurs, when you start out in the early years you will play close to the edge. This is why lots of businesses fail. The saying 'cash is king' is so true. Keep it tight and remember - run the business cash flow as if you were going out of business tomorrow. Never become complacent.

Although on the other hand, you must continually invest in your business for it to stay on top. I never said it would be easy!

Finding the right investor or business partner if you are going to go down this route is a big move, and you must get it right. Choose relationships and skill sets over money. I wouldn't want to be 'in bed' with someone who did not have a clue about business, as well as bundles of cash. Admittedly a lot of people probably would, but I am building relationships and a reputation that will go on for a long time. Know your exit, or how long the relationship will last. Some will want a quick in and out, but if you're planning long term this won't suit you.

I wanted an investor who shared my vision and philosophy on life. What I did not want was a jumped-up multi-millionaire I couldn't talk to or someone who would insist on telling me what to do. I know what I and my team can do, so I had a few options and I chose the right person for my company. I have to say I absolutely love the man who heads up the company that made an investment into Partyman, Philip Barton-Wright, who I mentioned earlier. Philip is a top bloke and as far as I am concerned, we need more people like him in the world. He is a great and wonderful chap who I look up to in every way. He is the perfect role model and a true gent, and he is worth far more than his bank balance because he has a heart of gold. I am fiercely protective of him, and I feel our relationship is living proof that business relationships can be about honesty and friendship.

When you give something up - and offering shares in your business IS giving something up - you will lose a part of what you have built. You must try and look at the bigger picture so you can accelerate your growth and learn a new skill set, and a super-experienced mentor who can teach you stuff you didn't know - that's a commodity you can't put a price on.

Find the right investor if you choose this route, and go by gut instinct and follow your heart – it's worked for me. I follow my gut in most of my choices in life, and if they go wrong - well, it makes my gut instinct better for next time.

Stay honest and never do anyone over, even when the relationship ends. If you decide to sell up and get out or buy back your shares, retire or clear off to the Caribbean, the relationship you have built can always be called upon in the future. The same with the bank - they are business partners in many ways, they take a debenture over the business so that if you sell they can get any money owed, but keep them sweet always, so if you need them they will come back. Which leads me on to my next topic:

Bank managers – finding them, changing them, keeping them

Here's my rule for bank managers – get a good one and keep him/her, but always change a useless one or one who can't get you what the business needs.

Without a doubt a good bank manager can get you to where you need to be a lot quicker, more so if you choose to go down the route of borrowing rather than approach an investor or venture capitalist - we still, as a business, rely on bank lending.

As I have said previously, getting a business off the ground is a big undertaking. Most businesses fail, and yours might too. If this happens you must learn, and grow stronger and better than before.

Ensuring you have the right skill set to combat failure is the way to go – whether it's your skills or someone else's, you will need the right manager, staff and accountant. But if you're going to borrow, then the right bank manager is essential. It's a two-way thing. For him or her to lend to you, you need to be able to comfortably show the right skills, budgets and accounts and demonstrate that you have a good team and a sound plan. Then you need to find out if the bank manager has the right skills for you.

In my opinion a banker has to be many things. First, they are providing you with a service - and believe me they really love lending to you when you don't need them to. Unfortunately this tends to be when the service is at its best. But in the early days it's a difficult game. The cash is tight, the profits (if any) are low and the stress is high, but at the same time it's great fun - if you're going in the right direction.

If you are new, things are tight and it's obvious you need help, a good bank manager will and should support you - I have had overdrafts of hundreds of thousands of pounds to get me through. I have had two great bank managers and to this day I still deal with them both. Ian at Lloyds TSB and Dave at Barclays Corporate both took a gamble on me, and I showed them my passion and how I was going to solve problems if I had them. I have also had a useless bank manager who gave me no help at all.

The good bankers will come and see you and talk to you and get to know your business, and they'll already know nearly every other business in the area. Both my great managers are like that. These guys really know what's going on and who's got what. They will line things up and network for you, champion you and help you in every way they can. They themselves are passionate about business and will try and work a way through a problem rather than cut you off. They know all businesses have good years and bad years, and they will take the long view.

You need a manager who will guide, help and support you through the good times and the bad. I am lucky enough to be able to call mine on his mobile - no call centre - and get a decision in principle or a 'no chance' on the phone, and he will see me within 48 hours over a cup of tea if I wish.

Bad managers will avoid leaving the office and won't be immediately straight with you if it's a 'no'. To be honest I'm sure there is a lot of rubbish out there that these guys see, and that's why banks have the famous 'no to loans' stigma, but if they see you have the skills, they will lend. I strongly recommend doing a little sole trader job before you start borrowing money - it will teach you the basics. And as I have said, learn basic accountancy. I'm not saying you should try to turn yourself into Warren Buffett, but banks love people who know their figures.

When you do make the big time, your bank manager will be able to work with you to advise on the best next steps for you. Remember that these guys will have had knowledge of businesses of all shapes and sizes, so ask them questions, and if they are good they will know the answers. I always ask how their other clients are doing. They can't be too specific because of confidentiality, but they can still give you useful information.

A key factor is how long they have been in the job - their experience is vital. Ask them for their comments on your ideas and plans - if I did this, would that work? What do you think of this? If he or she has been in the job a while their bank will value them more highly, and so should you. Both my managers have been in the job at the same banks for 25 years, nearly as long as I have been alive. Believe me they know their stuff - use it to your business's advantage!

Another thing I always ask is - what sign-off for lending do you have, ie who has to agree a loan? What is your relationship like with your credit control? Do you know the person who makes the final decision to lend, and how much influence do you have? If the answer sounds vague and wishy-washy, they may not know too much. I have always tried to get access to managers who are one tier up from me in terms of the sector I should be in – those who normally look after bigger businesses and bigger money than I deal in. Different people will look after small businesses, commercial and corporate, and the higher you go the better and more experienced the manager, as you would expect. I went straight into the commercial tier with my idea, then up to corporate as soon as I could. Spend your time finding out how your bank works and you will be well placed for the future.

Also make sure you click with them personally, so you can build a relationship which, if right, will become a strong and friendly relationship over the coming years.

Getting the right bank manager is a vital step on the route to success.

Raising cash summed up

One of the favourite things I like to say is that profit is not much use without the good old saying 'keeping the cash flowing keeps the business going'. That's really the way you as a business owner should be thinking.

1. Get up and go build the business - this will create turnover, and you need turnover to get going.
2. You then need cash flowing, because without it you are in deep trouble. Profit doesn't make one iota of difference if no one has paid you. Cash flow is the only way to service your debts, pay your staff and suppliers and the tax man.
3. Finally, you need profit.

When presenting to anyone, it's cashflow you need to understand more than anything. This will impress your potential partners, investors or bank manager - they know businesses have bad times and good times and many are seasonal. The entrepreneur who can say when his cashflow is going to be poor and understand why is the one who will survive and navigate the storms - and there will always be storms!

It's OK to have bad times with cash as long as you understand why, and know how to deal with it.

TOP TIP

Above all else in life, people want to buy from or buy into experts, so make sure you are perceived to be the expert in your field.

7.

UNDERSTAND MARKETING, AND WHY IT MATTERS

In my opinion, if you are not a marketeer or have a good understanding of the necessities of marketing, you will never reach super-success. To be a successful business owner or entrepreneur, you have to understand what marketing means, and if you don't know, you need to learn. Every day you must dedicate some time to marketing. If you're big enough to have a team doing this for you, it's important you look at what they're doing, and understand it so you can see that the team is following your objective. You need to be on the marketing team, in fact.

Every successful business owner is a marketer. There is a reason we all know who Walt Disney, Steve Jobs, Richard Branson, Mark Zuckerberg and Donald Trump are or were - they marketed themselves for the success of their brands and products, a trick I have picked up and done myself, as well as I can.

Nowadays marketing is much more complex than it was 20 years ago, but it's still fundamentally about matching a service or product to what people want and getting them to buy it – not just trying to sell something you happen to be good at producing. Luckily we now have the internet, which is brilliant for tracking and testing out what works. Years ago we relied on newspapers, leaflets, TV and radio, but the dotcom world opened up targeted audiences who search for your service. This means you can search for the exact type of customer you want, then target them - simply great for small businesses, because it gives them a chance to really compete. Marketing makes all the difference between good sales figures and lousy ones, and even the best sales team can't do their job if the marketing hasn't been done right. It's your job as a business to persuade customers to do business with you, then keep reminding them.

You will find that good businesses can get to a certain turnover or custom level with no marketing other than word of mouth. But at the next level of business growth, marketing to the right people can enable you to add the next tranche of turnover to propel the business forward.

Don't market for brand awareness, market to sell

It's easy to lose money with your marketing, unless you treat it as an investment and measure the return before spending too much. Marketing the brand without knowing the return on investment (ROI) might be OK for some of the big boys, not for us SMEs.

To market your brand for its own sake as the big international brands do, you really need to have deep pockets. If you are turning £100 million or less, then this should not be a strategy for your business. As business leaders and owners we should understand that we have to market to create sales - period. We are not in the realms of Coca Cola, L'Oreal, Facebook or Unilever. These are businesses with different agendas, which can afford to invest in brand awareness as well as running tactical sales campaigns.

I see myself (and our organisation) as guerrilla marketers or direct marketers, ie we market to people who love our product and have a high chance of buying from us. Any brand awareness I get from my marketing is a by-product - not the key objective.

Why should you market?

I was looking at buying a business just recently and the owners said they did some marketing when they had time, as if it was like switching the lights off at the end of the night! They just did not get it - marketing is indispensable, if you want your business to achieve sales.

It's so easy these days to measure the results – you can use the internet to help you measure your ROI, and you can also use it to look for ways of promoting your services. We are marketing our services every hour of the waking day.

Later in this book I will explain a key thing which I believe implements higher rates of success in business and marketing your business, and that's to put a 'mastermind' team together, a group of business owners who meet monthly. At the very least I strongly recommend you get together a selection of mentors, or build your network of experts around you. Once you have this you can share your marketing materials and get your peers to critique your marketing. You can then instantly implement your findings to improve your response on your marketing. I have dedicated a whole chapter to masterminds, mentoring and building networks – more on this subject later on in the book.

In this chapter I will hit on some marketing musts to get you going, but I plan to release a book in the coming year called *The Millionaire Clown's Marketing Magic*, which will be packed with super stuff to help you increase sales and profits.

One key thing businesses fail to understand is the difference between sales and marketing. The fact is, you need both, and without them you won't be able to breed 'magic' – or in this case, sales.

Many people think marketing is a fancy word for selling, but it's much more about matching what you can offer to what people want. Many business people fail because they invent a product which they assume people will want, then try to get the world to buy it, and guess what – they don't, because they don't need it, or there is already something out there that does the job better. Marketing starts with the buyer, not the seller. Identify an unfulfilled need or desire, then match it with a product or service you can deliver profitably, and you have a business.

Marketing generates the flow of leads into your sales operation so your sales team can convert them. No one wants to cold call – we all hate it, it's a waste of time and just drives people away. Create the interest through marketing, then push the leads to a super-hot sales team. It's much easier to get 1000 warm clients for a sales team to convert than pick up the phone to a load of unknowns.

To be a marketing magician you need these things to make your life easier:

1   A clear message that people can easily understand (don't tell them every little thing you do, they don't care, and too much information will drown out the key message).
2   Make them a compelling offer.
3   Give them trust - either testimonials or a brand they trust.
4   Above all, give them a product or service they love or want.

Let's look at some different marketing approaches. Bear in mind this is a whistle-stop tour of a subject that is worth a book on its own – or several.

Public relations

As you get bigger, an investment in PR could be a great one. If you don't have the ability or the time to write your own PR material or promote your product to the press, and don't have contacts in the key news media, find a professional who does. PR is a way to promote a product or service without paying for advertisements. To me this is the best marketing, because it works like word of mouth – you are getting others to say nice things about what you are offering. For this reason its value can far outweigh advertising.

In the early days I had to promote my Jimbo children's entertainer brand in ways I could afford. PR and word of mouth were my favourites, and getting local newspapers to run stories on our wonderful events was key. I would even make stories up or create stories for the press to follow. It's easy now to create stories for social media to follow. Instead of a business card I had fake money made with a picture of me on it, the telephone number presented like the serial number. It was a great way people could remember me by, and cheap. Remember, the internet was far less developed back then.

Now I use myself and my story of how a clown came to build a big business to get TV, radio and press stories for free, which in return all creates PR for the Partyman group. Keeping the Partyman brand in the press with positive news about its owner is a great way to get lots of free publicity which would otherwise cost thousands. This in return helps us create trust, and trust creates sales, because the business has a public face.

Build a database of prospects

If you don't have what modern marketeers call a 'list', or in layman's terms a database full of customers who do business with you or have shown an interest in doing so, you are most certainly losing out on sales. Many bright business marketeers even calculate how much they are prepared to pay for a lead. They will give stuff away to get a new customer, because they will do anything to increase the database – they know that a good new prospect could be a source of income for years to come. They make great offers to do this, and they work. They don't always have to involve discounting, either.

Supermarkets don't issue loyalty cards to say thank you for doing business with them, that's just what they tell you - the main reason is so that they can communicate with you, so they can track how much you spend with them, what you buy and when. Every time you swipe that card, they know about it. If you stop spending with them, they will post you an amazing offer to get you back. In fact they will go to any lengths to get you back in store, because the last thing they want is to lose you to another supermarket.

The big four supermarkets are competing on price, while the more exclusive compete on service and experience. Having you on a database, they know all about you and your habits and they use this to keep you coming back. It's super powerful stuff. Databases can track customers and give you a way to make them spend with you.

Now you're probably thinking that this is way too much for your business, but you can at least build a database, so you can start finding out who your customers are. It's cheap to do and will create sales. And you need to remind them to do business with you all the time - not once or twice a year.

TOP TIP

Make sure all your websites and marketing material, both on line and off line, have an option to create a database, even if it's just an email.

The marketing mix

Understanding the various aspects of marketing communication is essential. Let's have a look at current marketing trends at the time of writing.

The heading

What makes a newspaper sell, or a story make the front page? The HEADLINE! Make sure your marketing has a heading with your main message. I firmly belief that marketing should always be led by a heading rather than a shopping list of content that nobody will read. We call this the 80/20 rule - 80% headings, 20% content.

And don't fool yourself with a massive logo showing off who you are. Be more subtle with the logo and company name. A big company like CocaCola wants its name to be the main focus, but we as a small business want sales from our marketing. So in your heading, tell people what you are going to do for them with your amazing service or product. Separate the heading in a nice bold font behind another colour so it screams off the page over anything else in the marketing piece you have crafted. It's this heading that will then compel prospects to read your content and become customers.

Headings need prime real estate on your marketing piece, either on your website or offline.

The internet

As the internet evolves, its power in targeted marketing becomes more and more apparent. You can build a website and drive traffic to it or use Facebook and Twitter – there are all kinds of ways of getting business through the net. If you're not sure how to go about this, use an agency or bring in someone who does know. My top tip here is that you know what others are doing for you if you are not going to do it yourself, so take time to really understand what you are being sold to do. I myself have written many books on internet marketing and advertising - cheque books!

Understanding the basics of internet advertising and indeed marketing is a must on your list of learning for a successful entrepreneur. Remember, it's ever changing - what you know now is not what you will need to know in 12 months' time.

Mailshots and leaflets

A well-crafted leaflet with a strong heading, effective copy and a clear offer can return just as many customers for you on a cost per £1 basis as does direct mail, and if the cost and readership are good and your ad compelling enough, traditional print can work.

A really cheap way to see if a piece of marketing works and test its effectiveness is to ask people if it compels them to buy before you publish it or put it to the masses. Do your friends and family instantly get what you are saying? Is the message hitting home? Don't think that just because it's well designed it will hit home with your prospects. We all know when a shop is closing down that those crude hand-made signs with simple messages are sometimes the most effective. The clumsy handwriting and simple message attract people to go in and buy bargains that may not be available in the future. I try my marketing out on my team and other business owners in my circle to test their opinions. I call this my mastermind group (more about this later).

Mailshots written well can create sales. I tend to find that sending something through the post has power over emailing. Go back 20 years and people hated junk mail through the post, but now that we get less of it and more junk emails instead, a good sales letter can work well.

The mighty power of the offer

I notice that we always sell more when we add offers to our marketing. Your marketing should always contain offers, and they should include a 'call to action'.

Good offers are also key to creating first-time sales. If you want to win a new customer, give them an offer that's compelling. Once they buy, you have them. They will have learned that you deliver, and it's a lot easier to sell to people once they trust you.

There's much more to special offers than simply offering a discount. One of my favourites is the 30-day free trial - companies that provide TV subscriptions and membership systems simply say 'try us for 30 days absolutely free, then cancel whenever you want'. They know that if you like the service, you won't cancel. Guarantees, free goods or maintenance plans, consultations – they are all offers designed to win new customers.

Imagine you're a fruit and veg shop and you advertise a free home-grown bag of potatoes for every customer this Saturday. People will try it, and if you match it with service and a positive experience they will come back. You will gain customers for life.

Offers should always be about offering great value rather than simple discounts. It means so much more in the person's head - and discounting is not good for the bottom line, unless you are pricing high to discount down.

When we open a new day nursery, we offer a month's free childcare to get people to sign up - this can be worth up to £1000 to a family. If they sign up to a membership plan we give them VIP tickets worth £500 to a family for one of our events. This massive offer means much more than X% off and has a big impact, but we always put a short time limit on the offer, so people act straight away.

The call to action

The biggest failing of most SMEs in marketing communication is forgetting to close the sale by telling the prospect to take action NOW before they can go away and forget about it. This is the 'call to action'. With their busy lives we must get people to buy when they are looking at your services or products - you don't want them pondering whether to choose a competitor instead, or worse still thinking, 'I'll maybe do that later'. If you don't make them respond NOW, the moment has passed, the opportunity is gone, because they're thinking about something else. Here are some call to action examples:

Closing down today - buy now, we won't be here tomorrow!

Early bird price for the next 14 days!

It's just £99.95 till the end of the month but it will go up to £160 next month!

Limited supply – when it's gone it's gone!

Free book, CD or video course if you leave your email address here!

You should never extend the period of a call to action. There is no law about this, except the all-important law of faith between you and your customers. If you extend the call to action your customer will notice – and never trust you again. How often have you seen an offer continued long after it was supposed to have closed? It may work in the short term but customers are cute, they've seen it all before and they soon learn your limited offers are not limited at all. They know they have all the time in the world to order from you at the offer price, because the offer price is the usual price. So they relax, thinking maybe they'll get it next week or next month, and soon they have forgotten all about buying from you.

We all know the furniture shops that have a sale on all year round. They simply train their customers to think 'it's OK for us miss out on this offer, because this shop's offers never end'.

TOP TIP

You need to train your customers in how you do business and create a sense of urgency to act straight away through your marketing.

All it takes is a little reminder

Once you have a list of customers, remember that reminding them to do business with you makes all the difference between low sales and more sales. Just a nudge is sometimes all that's needed. People prefer to buy from brands that they know, like and trust, so just remind them of your latest product or service and tell them how you can help them. If you don't remind them to do business with you, someone else will.

So many business owners I know and deal with just don't do this. We have people we spend millions with as suppliers, and I'm sure that if they had a new product they could get us to buy it very easily, but they rarely bother to invite us to do so.

Lead generation

Everything you do must include lead generation. Every chance you get to communicate with customers, you should collect their details so you can communicate with them in the future. I even give stuff away to gain a customer or a lead. It's a trick that works really well. Remember people want to buy on a trust basis, and giving something away is a key to create trust. It has to be adapted to the business you're in of course – if you're a car dealer you don't want to be giving cars away for free, but maybe a weekend trial with a bottle of bubbly chucked in? I guarantee that the chances of the sale happening will be massively increased.

Discount third-party marketing

This works in terms of driving custom, but I hate it. The high discount sites such as Groupon and Wowcher have mastered the art of building a database of heavily-discounted products to get sales. The problem is that you get no profit from the sale, only turnover. Worse, you don't really get a customer either, because you are training the customer to buy purely on a discount basis – you will never be able to sell to them at a realistic profit. Discount third-party marketing is a dangerous thing. To me it's like a drug that gives a high, then a low. You're trapped by the need to continually offer more and more discounts just so you can sell to people who will never let you make any profit. Only desperate merchants who need short-term cash to survive can afford to join.

The only time discount marketing works is when you have a high margin product and are selling at an inflated price, knowing you are going to discount down through a compelling offer. Information-based products and seminars use this tactic to create sales. They are selling information, so they have high margin and can discount down easily and still make a bundle of profit. For example a headline price of £5000 down to £2,500 for information is not so bad.

Theme parks love to double ticket prices, knowing they can do two for ones or huge discounts to create a discount and drive footfall. Ultimately they get what they want, but only through inflating the headline price.

In summary, if you plan to discount down from the off through a high headline price this can work, but you want to control it yourself and not do it in a panic to get last-minute sales.

Joint ventures

Whenever two companies are directing different products at the same people, a joint venture is a great way to get to market. If you're a new business your partner can very quickly boost your sales - you just need to respect each other and build a good relationship. Joint ventures are a way to make some serious money in business, as you both bring something to the table.

Typically one partner has a database of hungry 'know, like and trust' followers who will be ready customers for the other partner's product. For example, say I have just brought out a great range of dog toys, but I need dog owners to sell them to. I approach a big dog food company and invite them to market the toys to all their customers in return for a percentage of the sales. I get instant sales without having to build my own database, while they get added profit for minimal investment. My toys may also help the sales of their dog food.

This happens all the time in the corporate world, with key brand leaders partnering up with suppliers to use the brands they own to leverage sales. Supermarkets have used their brands to create loan products, insurance packages and energy plans, all under their own name. People like to buy from brands that they know, like and trust.

Test and measure

Test and measure all your marketing, and dump anything that doesn't work. Online this is easy, because you can track traffic and results using Google's tools and cookies, which track visits. In the press, for very little money, you can put different phone numbers on different ads, so you can track where the calls are being generated.

The power of testimonials

All your marketing needs to include clearly-displayed testimonials or achievements accredited to your business. This creates trust and shows that people believe in you - and don't make them up, because people will know! If you can get pictures and a real life feel to them, the power will increase tenfold. Celebrity testimonials or those from trusted companies are very powerful – so are affiliations with government bodies.

The power of guarantees in marketing

Lots of people, when they buy something, get a thing called 'buyer's remorse'. They worry that they are wasting their money, or think they shouldn't have bought it. Offering product or money-back guarantees will ease people out of this place and make them feel better about buying from you.

TOP TIPS

You are a direct marketeer, tracking all spend as an investment.

Don't just do some marketing because everyone else does and you think it's all part of the routine - put some thought into it, and track the results. Marketing is an investment, and you must think of it like that.

If you know your place within the business, you will succeed, and that place is always to be involved in the marketing, no matter how big you get. I remember working with a florist I lent money too to set up her shop. She had a tough area to work from, so she struggled to get the business in, but she was great as a florist - she just didn't spend enough time going out to businesses and building a client base. Why? because she was IN the business and not ON it. Unfortunately her business went under. If you spend all your precious time IN your business, all you will do is save a wage rather than build a successful enterprise. Far better to become the marketer of your business, rather than the worker in your business.

8.

BECOME A BRAND TO CREATE TRUST

It doesn't matter how small or big you are - a by-product of your marketing, and indeed your business objective, should be to create a brand that will give a standard of instant trust to customers so that they buy from you over anyone else. This can be on a big or small scale. It's a misconception to believe that you need lots of time and money to create a brand. To be a brand leader in your sector locally, you just have to run a great business - simply put, you have to be known through your marketing to people who will buy from you. That marketing helps you to become a brand, but it's really the way you deliver your sale and how you look after your customers after the sale that will cement the brand in your customers' hearts and make them buy from you forever. If you can get this right and become a successful brand you will laugh all the way to the bank – though there'll be a lot of hard work on the way.

Picture the scene. You start a company that provides insurance called cheapinsurance.co.uk, quoting cut-price insurance for customers. Now imagine that on the same day a major supermarket like Tesco or Asda does the same thing. Their insurance actually costs more than yours, but that won't stop them having a multi-million pound business in year one, simply because of the huge brand they have built over the years. They might make a loss in their first year, partly because they'll invest millions in a marketing campaign to boost the launch of the new revenue/business line, but the point is that they have a massive head start simply because of who they are. And in years two and three, they'll clean up and make millions – at least they will if they get it right.

Look around us – brands are everywhere. We all live by them. Companies with successful brands know their immense value and use them to launch new businesses. Usually these are natural developments linked to the core business, like Disney moving from movies to theme parks to retail, cruise liners and holidays, but increasingly often the new business has very little to do with the original brand – look at Virgin. Richard Branson is the entrepreneur's entrepreneur. From the original company, Virgin records, set up in 1972, Branson has gone on to create a £5 billion multinational conglomerate with businesses in air travel, health clubs, mobile phones, trains, banking and finance, all called Virgin - the list goes on.

I love Richard Branson and the success he's achieved - he has even become a brand himself, with countless TV shows and books to underline it. You know what I love even more? The fact that when he was starting, some stupid city analysts said all this diversification was diluting his brand and told him to stick to what he was good at. He has proved them wrong. Virgin have got where they are today by talent-spotting companies they want to team up with. They supply the brand and the existing company supplies the operation. And now everyone's doing it – supermarkets being a prime example. It works because people know, love and trust their brands, because they feel they know what they are going to get. Watch a Disney film, then go to Disney World or take a Disney Cruise - you just know you're going to get the Disney magic all the way.

THE MILLIONAIRE CLOWN

You need to understand what your brand is. Think of it as a child. Look after it, stick with it and develop it, help it to grow. That's what we've done with Partyman. Just like the big boys, we have many branches on our tree, all carrying the Partyman brand. We like to think our customers see our brand and think 'funny, fun, good value but not cheap, great service, quirky, unique, give a cuddle and above all they trust us to deliver on the sale once they buy.

Of course, like all the big boys we have the brand signature look. Our colour is purple, and I feel at times that everything we do is purple. It's a colour that not many use and to me it carries a sense of magic. Even so, all that is tosh without the trust element our brand portrays. It has given us increased sales when we launch, because people know and trust us through our name.

Once people know you, they will recognise your language and traits. We use quirky language, and sign all our letters and emails 'magically yours'. Our staff are trained to be extra friendly and to remember that we are a 'yes' company. We try to source unique products and be first in the game. When we first set up our play centres we put on entertainment and built stages in our venues for the birthday cake and competitions - this was a first. It all goes to add to our brand building - keeping the trust consistent is the crucial task.

We cemented the Partyman brand for the towns we operated in. Hopefully as we inject our brand into more towns, people will get to know and love it and as we grow they'll use more of our services, like our online party shop. When people order we send them this great 'thank you for your order':

Partyman loves [name] for placing your magical order with us!

We were so happy that you ordered from us, we had a big party at the factory in celebration of you becoming one of our special customers!

We then printed your order and placed it on a velvet cushion for inspection by our lovely Partyman people, who work in our big purple factory to search for your party delights. Your ordered items were found and then hand picked off the shelf with the utmost care using purple sterilised marigold gloves! We then had a sad moment when we realised that the party goodies would be leaving us- that's how much we care! However, after a few minutes, we then remembered that they were going to a good home and will be used for the best party ever - yours!

Your order was then packed up, sprinkled with magic dust for a safe journey and all 50 of our Partyman staff jumped into the Partyman bus to the local Post Office, where each and every one of them jumped out and created a chain to pass your parcel one by one to the hands of the lovely postman, whose name was Trevor. We then all sang a little song as we wished your magical parcel a safe journey into your hands.

Your name is now up on our Customer of the Year board and we hope you visit our website again soon. If you ever want to call us for a chat to discuss your order or talk about how your day is going, please give us a call at 01268 661 503. We are real people working in our purple factory of fun, and love speaking to people!

Your order confirmation is below.

People love this, because they like the little touches we try and deliver on. They trust our brand to just do that, and we use people names in every order we do, to make it personal.

My point is - you must start on developing your image at the beginning and keep building on it. Ultimately, when building a brand, you're building a trust mechanism. People know what they will get when they do business with you. Marketers call this a KLT - know, like and trust.

Think of the things you love about companies you have dealt with and write them down. Then borrow their ideas, or the ones that will fit your company, and put your own spin on them - great delivery, service and product will come out.

There's a reason why concert tickets for top stars sell out in days of release - people trust the product - it becomes a brand.

Maybe you're a discount shop. You then need to make sure that everything about you says trusted value and economy. You're not the luxury brand. Know your place, stick to the same colours, fonts and wording in publications and stick to the product you are offering. Remember you are creating a trust basis which you will deliver consistently on the brand you're building.

Know what your company is all about, stick to the brand and the word will spread. Back it up with marketing and testimonials and the advice in my other key chapters, and you have a business with WORTH.

You don't have to have millions to build a brand, as long as you start right - start small and grow. I started the Partyman brand as a clown and it grew and grew, but we still use the brand values I built when I was 16. If you are loud and love life like me, it's a great idea to use yourself as a front for the brand. People will trust this, and it's great the amount of free publicity this will get you. This approach isn't for everyone, but if you feel comfortable, do it. It worked just fine for me - after all, I was in the entertainment industry.

I have all our vehicles sign-written - not to get work directly, as I am sceptical about this working, but to keep reminding people of the brand. The more they see it, hopefully the more they will trust it. That's why when you watch a football match you see all those brand names displayed around the pitch. You're not going to buy a new phone while you're watching the match just because you see 'SAMSUNG' flashing at you, but it'll help to plant the idea in your mind that Samsung is BIG and therefore the best, the one to go for - it creates TRUST. We make sure all our letterheads, websites and uniforms are obviously Partyman. This is a key lesson. Build a brand from little acorns and watch it grow into a huge, strong oak tree that we can all trust. That trust is what will make people spend money with you over weaker brands that don't have the same trust factor.

TOP TIP

Remember - you can't just build a brand with a memorable name or quirky marketing and brand design alone. It needs to be matched with trust that you will provide outstanding customer service and delivery of your offer, service or product. A great brand = trust!

9.
HOW MULTIPLE REVENUE STREAMS MAKE YOUR BUSINESS STRONGER

Multiple revenue streams, or multiple streams of income, are just fancy ways of saying that you don't rely on income from one source – because that source might dry up, and then you'll have nothing to fall back on. Every business should have money coming in from more than one source.

As an individual you need to be putting some salary away to build for a second or third revenue stream that does not need your time, something that creates revenue as you go rather than when you're old, like a pension. This revenue is what we call passive and residual. At the end of this chapter we can look at the options on how to do this from an individual.

Partyman as a business is just one of my income lines - I have property income, entertainment income and now sales from my book, along with information-based products and public speaking too. Our business income flows are all connected to brands that families love, which makes them work more effectively. Partyman boasts 10 income streams, all producing cash flow to help us to pay our staff and meet our goals. We get income from admissions, laser arenas, food and beverage, childcare, online sales, retail, entertainment, events, play centres, membership and venue hire. Each stream gives us insurance for the others. Whatever business you are in, you can do the same. You'll find life gets easier that way. We have done it in every department and every business we have created. When we bought our farm adventure park, we added a new restaurant and an events business within nine months, with a childcare arm planned and on the way.

We did it with our play centres too. We added nurseries and laser arenas, so we get three revenue streams from one venue.

If pubs had not thought about adding food, where would they be today? Even more of them would have closed. The wise ones added function rooms and converted back rooms to B&Bs – that's four revenue streams. Farmers build fishing lakes or open farm shops, while a builder might add a decorating arm.

Examples:

Café - start doing door-to-door catering or take-away food.

Hotel - add meeting rooms and business suites.

Gym - add a nursery or a café, or both.

Estate agents - offer lettings as well as sales, plus maybe a building service.

The supermarkets could offer insurance, loans, clothes, mobile phones, holidays, health care, pensions, a pharmacy - oh wait, they already do! And the strength of the brand allows them to succeed, instantly and on a huge scale.

The value of property

To me property is a good place to put spare cash in if you or the business does not need it, and invariably it takes up less of your time. Without doubt, property has helped me to achieve three things in life:

1 A contribution to residual income
2 Capital growth in its value
3 The ability to borrow from the banks to grow my business.

That last one is by far the most important. Thank God I started buying property early on to achieve this. Along the way through my business life I have met property owners who have told me that with property you can lead a finance-free lifestyle in just 12 months by creating a passive income, without money. It just isn't that simple. You do need money to start a property portfolio - property needs money for a deposit and then you need to buy right and look for a good yield. A discount at purchase will give you an immediate chance of growth in capital. I always believe that the profit made in property is made the day you buy, by buying right.

You will by rights make money over the long term as the property appreciates in value - but this is not a two or three-year plan, it's a whole life plan, in effect a pension plan. As it grows in value you can remortgage, release cash and buy more to grow your rental income, should you wish.

Don't overstretch yourself, and do follow these basic rules:

1 Buy for rental yield first, capital growth second - you want to be able to pay your bills and have something as you go along.
2 Buy right - negotiate the best deal, not what you think looks nice.
3 Make sure it's going to be easy to rent out (location is key).

Property is the stuff banks love to lend against. It gives you options, opens doors and raises your wealth index score. Money in the bank seems pointless to me as it depreciates in value (unless you get a massively high rate of interest, and I mean 20%), so if you have money, property to me is a safe bet, if you don't plan to sell it and you buy right. For example, if you have £100k in the bank, after a year it would pay you circa £5k at a rate of 5%, and that's if you're lucky enough to find such a high rate of interest.

Recently I found a property deal which with a £100k outlay (the deposit) would pay me a rental of £50k per year. I would also have a £400k mortgage, but over time the property would go up in value and the rents pay my debt down and pay me a lovely return. So let's work this out:

Rent in - £50,000

Mortgage, including paying down the debt (capital, not just interest) -

£33,000

Annual balance received - £17,000.

So if I have £5000 worth of bills, which is the worst case, it would still leave me £12,000 clear profit to pay my taxes, or go on a nice holiday, or put towards the next property.

The above figures were worked out on a commercial property paying the capital down and paying off the interest, but a lot of property investors choose to pay just the interest, as it's more tax efficient in the UK. Paying down capital is seen as income and therefore generates a tax bill every year.

Sadly, banks want you more and more to pay down capital on commercial property. However on the upside, in 15 years it will be yours, lock stock and barrel.

So in summary, my £100k in the bank has conservatively returned three times more cash than it would in the bank. Plus, the property appreciates in value every year (as long as we don't have a property crash), so to me it's a much better bet.

I would imagine this property will be worth at least £1.2 million in 15 years, so that's a £700k growth - plus it would have paid me circa £765,000 in rent with £225,000 in rental profit. So at the end of the 15 years I would have been able to pay back all I owed, giving me a clear £1.2 million plus my £225,000 rental profit, making £1.425 million on my £100k investment. My £100k in the bank would be worth £212,000 if I did nothing at the end of the 15 years. And remember, that £200k is going to be worth a lot less in 15 years than it is now.

The moral of the story is - make your cash work hard, just as you do.

10.
WHY RESIDUAL INCOME IS THE FANDABBYDOZY OF BUSINESS GOALS

This is the most important piece of advice I can give you as a business person, bar none. Residual or passive income is the money that comes in every month regardless of what you do. Usually it's not as profitable as a one-off sale, for example buying a car, but here's the thing - it keeps coming. Wouldn't you like thousands of customers paying something every month into your bank account? Imagine the ease it will bring to your life. Sky TV, house insurance, membership, electricity, internet – to you they are all outgoings, but to your supplier they are priceless residual income. All these people have to do is keep providing a good enough service to keep their customers, and it never stops.

Residual income stops you chasing turnover every month. I have invested heavily in time and money in building it for myself and my business - in fact it has saved my business. My aim is that my residual income line in my business should pay all my staff, rent, rates and loans every month, and I am already half way there.

When I opened my first play centre, I opened the doors and people came in. I let people know we were there, and everything was lovely. It was easy to get everyone in, because it was new. But then competition came along, and we had to work harder and smarter to keep our customers and get new ones. It also became apparent that my turnover was wavering up and down, so I started working on multiple revenue streams to protect us. I was determined that I would have a residual income in the business to help me sleep at night. I hated having to keep my fingers crossed that business would come in, because it could be affected by the weather, holidays, kids at school - it pissed me off. So I decided to open a day nursery. I had built up a network of contacts in business and a good friend of mine, Paul Sharp, had done just this. Four years on we turn £120,000 a month on childcare, and within two years it will have grown to a third of our income. It grows by 20% every year and the cash lands in our bank regardless of weather, holidays – anything. At last my leisure and entertainment business had a residual income - it was magic!

Thank God I networked and networked again - otherwise I would never have been able to implement this.

So now I am residual income obsessed. It's a surefire way of building a great business. I was not sure how I could do this in a leisure business at first and I was racking my brains trying to think how, but then I had an idea – we could become like a gym and charge people a monthly fee to visit us. I knew a couple of people who were doing this and it seemed OK. In fact when we took over a business in Stevenage they had 400 people signed up, and I had to let them all go because our systems could not accommodate them. I had to work to sort that out.

Then through my network of contacts I went to one of the smartest blokes I know, Andrew Wolfe, who I mentioned earlier. Andrew is a real inspiration to me - in fact he may not realise it, but I am a little in awe of him. His attitude, his fair approach, his ability to help others and his happiness make him a super businessman and a thoroughly nice bloke. Andrew is also a business turnaround king who knows how to set up a great team to build a great business that was losing cash hand over fist until he took over, and he is someone I very much model myself on.

Andrew generates half his customers from a membership system for his farm park, which makes him the busiest farm park in the country. It's not appropriate for me to tell you what he gets in residual income, but I can safely say its impressive, and customers love what he does.

Thanks to Andrew, I am close to implementing my second residual income stream to the business, aptly called 'Partyman's Magic Pass'. This will create a great value membership system, allowing my guests to pay from just 23p a day for unlimited use of all our attractions, laser arenas, Partyman Worlds and Marsh Farm Animal Adventure Park, plus anything else we open. What's more, we guarantee we will freeze the price you pay for the life of your membership to reward loyalty, and you'll get 15% off all food, drinks and retail. I'll also add a call to action to sign up now with a massive offer that adds value, like tickets to one of our events. It's going to be massive, and it will be a vital part of our turnover every month.

So thanks to Andrew I realised through my network of contacts that I can have a residual income in leisure. And to be fair, because I have a chain of leisure businesses I can make the offer even more attractive.

Here are some ideas for building residual income into your business:

You're a builder who has built a house?

- Offer a maintenance plan which provides three tiers of service level.
- *You're a jobbing gardener?*
- Pay us £x a month and we will look after your garden for a year.

You run a restaurant?

■ Start a membership scheme so customers get invited to exclusive member nights which include your food.

You run a sports shop?

■ Come to an arrangement with a local sports centre to offer your customers discounted membership on which you take a profit.

In essence, customers who pay you every month regardless will make your life easier, build value and give you reliable cash flow.

Also remember what I said about finance – it's cash flow that keeps a business going, NOT profit. You can make a million pounds profit on a deal but if the customer doesn't pay for six months – where does that leave you? Simply put, if the cash doesn't flow you won't stay in business.

TOP TIP
Keeping the cash flowing keeps the business going.

11.

LEARN BASIC ACCOUNTING AND CASH FLOW

Don't do your own accounts – it's time-consuming and boring – BUT you do have to be able to understand them. You need to know what things cost, and act as if you have no money all the time – it'll keep you grounded. This is the difference between success and failure. If you just act like an accountant, you will never take the risks that go with driving a business forward.

Accountants are a funny breed - they think they always know best, but of course, they don't. They are advisors, not decision makers. However you do need them, and you need to understand the figures they produce before you make the choice to take another risk, acquisition or growth plan.

To fight your corner and evaluate what you want to do for attracting bank loans or investments - or indeed using the company's cash, or your own for that matter - you need to understand what it's going to cost.

It amazes me how many business people don't know what management accounts are, don't know how much profit they are making each month, or even worse, how much they are losing. My turning point in my business was when I got to grips with the accounts. I can argue my corner without an accountant now to get what I want, and once you get to that stage, your business will improve.

Now as my accounts team know, I haven't a clue how to enter an invoice in Sage or even log into our accounts software, but they know. And they know that by the beginning of next month I'm going to want the previous month's figures so I can track departmental profit and loss.

I also have the bank balance figures sent to me every morning - remember that what's in the bank is not the same as what's yours. At the click of a button I can see the amount we are owed and the amount we owe to others.

I get staff to try and run little profit and loss checks for their departments. I know if a department is making a loss and costing us cash, and I know it's my choice to carry on investing in it, spend more time in it or cut it out. Usually I try to keep things going so they do eventually turn in our favour, but monthly accounts will give you a better business and enable you to see any financial problems your business has. If you ever get to the stage where you can get weekly updates, that's great, and if you can tie them up to a decent set of projections, even better. I must also say that the business owner should do the budget forecasts – it's your chance to work out where you will be and give yourself realistic targets to hit.

Knowing your figures is key. Signing all the cheques, checking the bank statements and questioning every pound that's spent is demanding, but in fact it can be quite fun.

Twice a year I'll get together with a few of the team to have a 'check the suppliers' day and we always save money as a result. But don't cut costs so much that you lose value - this is a mistake I have made. Understand the difference between cost and investment for the business to make it bigger and better. The nature of the beast is that the more you turn over and the bigger you get, the more waste you get. It is going to happen - get used to it, but at all costs keep a lid on it.

We now spend £2.5 million on wages a year. If I could save just 5% on this bill I would make £125,000 extra net profit - but would the cuts damage my overall plan? That's why an overall objective is important. Does spending this money help us to achieve the objective, or am I just concerned about what I am making this month?

By doing monthly figures I know if we have overspent or had a bad month, and I can see where I need to make changes for the months ahead. I take this one step further - I share our accounts every month with all my managers. This gives me a chance to see them all and help us network with each other. They need to know if the news is good or bad. If it's good, they feel great about working for a company that's doing well and will give them a career path - if it's bad, we can think about what we need to do to change it moving forward.

I can honestly say that this was how my business career changed, knowing figures. I know how much we turn a month, how much we make, lose and spend, and I can also see any mistakes we make in the accounts. It's one of the differences between Oxes and business magicians - Eagles.

Even if you only make a few hundred a week, do a little mini profit and loss sheet. The people who just give boxes of receipts to their accountant every year (that used to be me) will have to wait till after the year end to find out what they are making - or not. Do it yourself first, then get the accountant to do it properly at your year end.

You should also run budgets for yourself and the team, which will enable you to hit the targets you want to hit. Do it on a spreadsheet. If you are a new start-up and you want to open a coffee and cake shop and are to be VAT registered, decide what you are worth a year - at present the average wage in this country is around £26k - and then add on £30k net profit. You will be working hard, so you need to make it worth your while, and you need to make the net profit to invest in the business and keep the bank happy.

Ask yourself if you know what EBITDA (Earnings Before Tax, Interest, Depreciation and Amortisation), net profit and gross profit are, because you can bet your bottom dollar your bank manager does, and the start of getting out of problems or borrowing cash to grow is your banker. If he believes in you then you have a fighting chance, but you have to have the right tools for him to believe in you (see Rule 3).

You need to ask your accountant questions and learn the basics. You can then direct him or her on what you want doing. These people are far more used to obtaining finance than book-keeping - get a book-keeper to do that, not an accountant.

Say you want to open a coffee shop. Tell your accountant 'I want to open a coffee shop and it's going to cost me £150k to set up and I have £75k, I want you to get me the rest from the bank'. Then put your business plan together and your projections, because even if you hate this stuff and find it boring you *must* understand it.

Imagine you start with 12 months and put in the predicted lines of income for that period. Don't forget to knock 20% off your takings for VAT if you turn over more than £81k in a year (2014/15). Talking of VAT, if you're a small business this is the killer. It's taken me seven years to get used to VAT, or sales tax as our friends in America call it - in the UK it's the invisible shareholder that takes 20% of your business. Always remember that 20% of what goes in the till is not yours. I hate VAT and have campaigned at Parliament and written to MPs to try and get it down in the leisure sector. For me it's unfair, because I feel that our customers in our sector don't appreciate that we have to pay 20% out. I would much rather we be like America and do everything plus sales tax rather than include it in the cost of the sale. It's unfair the way it just keeps on increasing.

TOP TIP

Know your monthly figures, and better still if you know the weekly figures - it will change the way you do business!

12.

IF YOU'RE THE SMARTEST PERSON IN THE ROOM, YOU'RE IN THE WRONG ROOM

Getting the right mindset for super-success is a priceless asset. The more you learn, the more you earn – it's simple.

From my very early days of business I was naturally drawn to people who were doing better than me, and not just in my business sector. In a way these people became mini-mentors. Mentoring works – it's a way of getting where you want to quicker.

One of the things I have noticed in my business life, and life generally for that matter, is the simple fact that who you hang around with is who you become. If you hang out with people who take drugs, spend all the money they earn as soon as they get it and lead wasted lives, there's a good chance you'll end up wasting your life too. Spend lots of time with super-successful people and guess what, you have a much higher chance to become super-successful too.

That's where the title of this chapter comes from. If you really are the smartest person in a circle of business owners you're chatting to and getting advice from, change your circle. Look for Lions and Eagles - or Oxes who want to become Eagles.

Now folks, this is not just my thinking - this is the thinking of great entrepreneurs. It was first expressed by the author of the book *Think And Grow Rich*, Napoleon Hill. He researched 40 millionaires to see just why they were so much more successful than others. His findings showed that these people all had certain habits in common. One of them was the ability to share ideas and plans.

Going forward with this ideology, I believe we as entrepreneurs really need to set up those mastermind groups I talked about in the marketing chapter. These are like boards of directors from different companies who meet to discuss how they can make all their businesses better. Imagine doing this on a personal development basis for the businesses that don't have boards or massive teams yet.

You need to do this with people outside your business. The beauty is that you can all hold each other accountable for what you said you would do the last time you met. It keeps you focused and driven to achieve. Only recently I took my foot off the accelerator for a few weeks and saw our sales start to slip. The brainstorming and collaboration between up to eight people who are better or as good as you in the very least will drive you - and them - up the ladder. You also instantly gain a support group giving you skills, experience and confidence.

You must make sure when you set up your mastermind that the people round the table have similar interests, skills and at least the same success levels or more, as well as clear visions and goals and a desire to make changes to reach the above. People who join your group must have the unanimous consent of all the others in the group, so it has a good, happy feeling, because they should be fun!

Before you create your mastermind, you must at the very least have the following:

1   A business mission statement, or personal vision.
2   A list of your 1-year and 5-year goals.

3   A place to have these meetings, because you need to make sure they happen. I would always try to do it in a different place each time and on a rolling calendar, so the members take turns to book the mastermind each month.
4   All members must ask themselves and all those in the mastermind why they should be chosen to for the group - even if it's your idea and you prompt the action.

It's super-powerful stuff that can really make you get things done.

In many ways business is like sport. Train and play with the best, and you play better than you will if you play with a load of second-raters. Remember - the best teachers at school got the best out of the class.

Business coaches

Business owners, like sportsmen, can benefit greatly from coaching. I have heard nothing but good from people who do it – seriously, people do really well from it. Coaches will coach you to be great. I have had sit-downs with a few coaches over the years. It may be stuff you already know, but coaches constantly keep you on it and hold you accountable on stuff you have not done that you said you would. This can get you places a lot faster and more successfully.

Mentors

A one-to-one arrangement with a mentor can be of enormous value. I've been lucky enough to have some great unofficial mentors, as mentioned above, and I wouldn't be the businessman I am without them. A mentor can share with you their wisdom and experience across different fields of business over many years. I've now begun to offer counsel to business owners all the time, and I love it!

THE MILLIONAIRE CLOWN

My mentors have not been officially hired as mentors – they are just wise people who I can go to for advice. They have enabled me to achieve my goals in a much shorter time, all through learning and listening to them. They have helped me to give all the people we employ a job and a livelihood. Sometimes you may not even realise that you are being a mentor, or that you are being mentored. Many people who meet me think I am just a big clown, a buffoon who doesn't know much. Compared to some of them, perhaps I am!

Remember, there's no point in being the smartest person in the room. When you are with people who know more and have achieved more than you, it may be the time to shut up and listen. In that situation it's not your achievements that matter, it's theirs. So in these situations, I don't play the bighead or the know-all. I listen and take it all in. They have been to places I haven't been, done things I haven't done – yet.

Of course, you need to know who will make a great mentor. Not all successful business people are wise, and not all the wise ones will be able to pass their wisdom on to others. Some highly successful people think they know it all because of their success in one particular field, which may have been achieved partly through other people's skills or investment, through their own exceptional knowledge or experience in that field, like a retired racing driver making money from racing car design.

If you're a business owner sharing advice, helping people should be a part of what you do - it goes both ways. I go to schools and universities and help as many as I can to become business owners and leaders.

I humbly thank all those who have helped me. I thought it would be jolly good to list all the mini-mentors who have helped me as I have grown up, to explain how they have helped me – you might be able to do the same thing.

Firstly, my **Dad**. He gave me the property bug and without knowing, made me realise he had multiple revenue streams.

Colin Whymark from the café where I first worked taught me how to deal with customers and manage multiple businesses.

Craig Gallimore showed me how to make a success out of children's entertainment and helped me to set up my first business.

Mat Mason explained to me about the food business, VAT and staff, and helped me through the dark days when business was tough. He also showed me how to set up my first venue.

Ian Douglass was my first business bank manager, a wonderful man who helped in my early days.

Dave Oram is my other bank manager. He has been fantastic in giving advice and helping me to make things happen

Steve Shaw was a trusted rock who helped me set up my cash flows and accounts.

Andrew Wolfe has indirectly been a great inspiration to me in recent years for all the wisdom and tips I have listened to and ultimately I have then implemented.

Philip Barton-Wright is a truly successful businessman who helped me get where I wanted to go a lot quicker than I could have done alone - because he believed in me.

I hope I have done you all proud, and thank you for everything. I also hope that in the future the experience I have gained from my achievements - and my mistakes - will help others in the quest to build a business, through my services as a mentor and through seminars to help business owners.

TOP TIP

Managing risk is critical to success - but don't overcomplicate stuff. Keep it simple, but don't do it until you've done a little homework – not too much homework, otherwise you may never get anything done!

The Rules Of Success

13.
CONSISTENCY, CONSISTENCY AND MORE CONSISTENCY

It's what McDonalds pioneered before anyone else - the idea that you can be in Hong Kong, London or New York and walk into the same restaurant. Achieving the same branding, marketing, price, service and food on a global scale as they have done is nothing short of a business marvel. It means each store markets the others. The likes of Starbucks, Disney and Holiday Inn have all managed to achieve this too.

Consistency is the only way to build a super-strong business. You should also know the level of consistency you will deliver. There's room for McDonalds/Tesco/Starbucks consistency and then there's room for Disney/Hilton/Rolex consistency - let me explain.

Most small businesses I come across have a key man, an entrepreneur behind the whole thing. This girl or guy has either seen or worked in a business in the same sector and thought 'I could do this better'. But can they deliver on it consistently? Will the team be as good as the boss?

I was lucky - I had a few great staff from day one at Partyman, and with my key team I could do it. So when I was in the business and my key team was operating in our early days, we delivered good experiences. Our consistency was of a high-class business with a low-class price tag - in effect you were getting a Disney service at McDonalds prices. But this raises two problems - it's not sustainable because it's not affordable, so making this work relied on me and my key team, and this could have held back the growth of the business. But if you can keep this consistent, customers will love it, and in our case it worked. I said I wanted to grow the business and I was on the hunt for new opportunities. This did make consistency suffer and our customers started to say we weren't delivering the same service – it wasn't as clean and looked shabby.

Here's some key simple rules to get consistency into your business.

1 **Decide what business class you are**, and if it's basic then stick to it – don't try to go upmarket. McDonalds and Easyjet are great at this, and let's be honest, none of us would mind just 1% of their annual income.

   If it's a luxury, high-end business you want - Disney or Rolex - then you're into the realms of experience delivery. Why do people not mind paying twice as much for an Apple computer as a PC? It's the experience - the great in-house stores, with amazing staff, the sleek design, the stunning brand, the box, the experience of saying 'I bought an IPad', not just 'I bought a tablet'. Apple have created such a great experience that they can charge double for it, and customers are happy to pay. I for one will always pay Apple the extra money for the experience of buying and owning the stuff they make, all the more so because I know it's consistent. Consistently fabulous in fact. Most retailers would love to achieve what Apple make per square foot of retail space!

2 **Plan from day one** if you want to be able to roll out the business, and keep the experience consistent once you do this. If you're a

small business you need to work out how you can keep it consistent on your days off, or when you're on holiday.

3 **Get it down on paper** as soon as you can. And if that's not you, get someone else to get it down on paper for you. I'm writing this book partly so that the wider world can benefit from my experiences. Get a business plan that outlines what your business is and where it's going to be from birth to five years, then ten. Business plans help you achieve consistency - they are not just for the bank and a way to borrow money. Once you have yours, circulate it among your people, get their views. Most importantly, your managers and staff should know it inside out, upside down and round and round.

4 **Marketing, branding and personality** must all be consistent. If your colours are purple then they must stay purple, not bluey-mauve or purpley-red (colours have numbers – find out what yours is on a colour reference system such as the Pantone Matching System and give the number to everyone who wants to reproduce it). **Use the same colour and the same font everywhere**, on stationery, vehicles, staff contracts, websites, flyers, business cards, clothing and so on. Your logo too has to stay consistent – once you've developed a good one, keep using it. Many small businesses keep on fiddling with their corporate look, changing logos and fonts and so – these days with computers it's too easy, and too tempting. But you will just confuse your customers and your team. Remember that your customers don't see your logo many times every day as you do – at the point when you're beginning to feel bored with it and wondering if it needs changing, they are probably just beginning to get used to it and to recognise it and what it stands for. Just think about Innocent, Virgin, Starbucks, Dreamworks - you know instantly from the branding that it stands for the consistent products or services you love. Branding may need to be updated

occasionally, but unless you're trying to reinvent a fading brand and tell the world you've changed, never make a sudden drastic change, because customers won't recognise the new livery and you'll lose all that goodwill and trust.

5 **Price consistency** is mega-important for consumers. They need to know you're affordable, and that's fine, but don't keep trying to be cheaper and cheaper – it won't be sustainable and it's not necessary. Again if you're premium-priced that's fine too, but customers need to know why – you need to keep offering a consistent experience. Coffee from Starbucks has a huge mark-up and we all know it, because we know we can make a cup of coffee for a few pence at home, but put in smartly-dressed baristas, comfy sofas, beautiful aesthetics and the correct lighting and people will happily pay three or four pounds to drink your coffee.

In our business we are trying hard to deliver consistency in businesses we take over as well as in our own. We do it by offering the same menu, the same branding, the same coffee, the same flooring, the same paint colours, the same uniform, the same way of answering the phone, the same customer experience, the same aesthetics, the same music, the same furniture - and damn, we even try for the same smell! We recognise that through this consistency we can develop our staff, use the same business plan, benchmark against each site and raise standards.

Tips for consistency implementation:

Problem: 'My staff work really well some days but not so well on the other days, and some of the staff are better than others.'

Solution: Consistent staff delivery is essential. Use constant training and reinforcement to ensure that everyone is up to scratch, and make sure your managers understand the importance of consistent performance. If standards are falling on some days, ask yourself why. McDonalds do this brilliantly, and they don't pay big bucks to staff, mainly because their consistent staff training and operations ensure they achieve this.

Get better at recruiting. Are you recruiting your staff the right way? We hire for our leisure business on personality, not CVs, because that's what the leisure business needs. We audition, not interview, and we advertise for 'cast members', not staff, to work for us.

If the work is more office based, ask for them to do a trial day first, and observe the way they function. And provide good staff training, development and career prospects - this will encourage them to be more consistent and know they have a goal to aim for.

You need systems and processes - you will find life easier and your team will be that much more efficient. Get that operations manual in place for whatever business you run, because if it's not written down and made part of your system, you'll never have a bigger model to roll out!

If you take anything from this book, please don't let yours be a great business when you are there to look after things and then just an OK business when you're not. Don't take the attitude 'I can't leave the business because no one does it as well as me', because that's where you'll stay. Start building your business from day one so it can go on running consistently without you in it. Only you can make this happen.

When people come to you with ideas, ask: is this going to be a consistent experience for the business? Not just for your team, guests or customers but for suppliers too. Suppliers need to be consistent - imagine if Starbucks could no longer get the bean that makes their coffee. Can you imagine what all those millions of customers would think? Taste consistency is paramount to them, so suppliers need to be consistent for customers to carry on buying.

We in our business are trying every day to be known as the customer experience champions, knowing that whenever the public decide to interact with our business we offer not just a service but a consistent experience of fun, care, education and happiness. To this end we are creating Magic Makers, a team of great cast members (not 'staff', remember) who have become producers and choreographers for the rest of the cast to come up with magic ideas to apply to our business. They will add customer experience to the team (not service but experience), and instill our ethos, audit and praise. This costs money, but it's essential for the longer view.

Invest in consistency from day one.

14.
BUILD A NETWORK, AND KEEP NETWORKING

Overlook this one and you're missing out on success big time, because as they say - 'It's not what you know, it's who you know'.

Networking has given me the very best opportunities in my business career and in the Partyman journey. Very early on I learned that meeting new people in the business world was a key part of getting on in life. It does help that I love doing it. Meeting people is something I enjoy like nothing else. I have made great friends, recruited great staff and got great leads for the business by getting good at this - and the only cost is a little of your time. I can honestly say that if I didn't network and put the time into exercising my people-meeting skills I wouldn't have my business, or the life I have today.

So in the early stages of a business, how do you do your networking? In the beginning you have to go out there and find the opportunities. Do you have a trade body for your industry? Join it! You will meet other people in your sector who can give you tips and ideas. You'll be amazed how many established businesses will help people starting out - and so they should.

Chambers of Commerce and local councils often hold meetings

for local businesses - get yourself along. Our local council even had a business networking version of speed dating, so you got to meet 50 local businesses in an hour. All this was free, and we picked up a client worth £20k a year!

Join local business awards schemes, go to breakfast meetings and ask your bank if they hold business networking meetings – another way your bank manager can help. They can do a lot more than just lend money.

I have just been to a three-day away trip to other theme parks with 130-plus visitor attraction owners. We shared contacts and accounts, ideas and marketing tips, and I'm ready to go and implement all these new ideas into my new business. It gave me a chance to really focus on the business with other owners.

Networking for business

Sometimes it takes a couple of years to get actual business from a networking contact, but it can be well worth the wait. Often when I meet new people nothing happens for a while, but then three years later I get a call, and the next thing I know I've made the best deal I have ever done.

Networking for learning

When you're networking it's not just about selling your wares, it's a chance to learn. You pick up so much more than you realise. I am bold, I always ask questions and on many occasions I send my accounts to people I have met, so we can compare costs. You'll be surprised to learn that a lot of business owners, once they get off their high horses and stop telling you how great they are, will tell you the good, the bad and the ugly about the enterprise they run, but you have to meet people and create a circle of contacts for this to work.

Networking for your team

I found my best team members through my networking, either through knowing people or meeting new people. They have often gravitated towards us, or us to them, through social contact, networking and meetings. Here's a fact for you - all my top team have been found this way, without a single recruitment company used or a single job advertisement.

Network for friends

I have got so many friends in business, and I am proud of that. My business has allowed me to meet great, inspirational people who have become great friends.

So get out and network, now.

15.
BUY A FAILING BUSINESS AND MAKE IT GREAT

I have to say many people have labelled me as a bit of a business turnaround king - thanks, very nice of you. In fact it was never intentional, at least not at first. Then, as I accidentally slipped into this model, I grew to understand it, and I have created some great opportunities from it.

It can be hard at times, as you'll face problems in abundance. You'll need a positive attitude that gives you the ability to steer a big ship out of troubled waters. However, without this strategy my business would not be where it is today. I have acquired businesses and sites that have been in tremendous financial trouble and I have rebuilt them from scratch. Rescuing failing businesses has enabled me to get to new markets quicker with lower costs, and in many cases I have picked up businesses with little investment in cash at the time of acquisition. This has included buying businesses that have actually gone bust, being in administration or liquidation at low prices, or even for nothing.

Remember what I said earlier about keeping overheads low and debt to a manageable amount? It's a key factor in making money easier. We are super strict in making sure we negotiate the best terms for our business so we can control overheads to keep them as low as possible.

So in summary, get out there and look for a failing business that you can pick up cheap, which just needs some rules implemented. Usually they need TLC, systems, marketing and management, rather than just cash. It's a great way to increase your business.

It can take longer to turn a bad business round if you're not making visible change. Buying a failed restaurant and implementing great new menus and customer experience will take a while to feed through to the masses. A relaunch with new name, decor and customer service may be needed too.

There is no such thing as a free lunch, of course. Your time and turnaround efforts will be needed, but it can save you money over starting from scratch – remember the customers who are already using the business will love the improvements you make.

You're probably itching to know how I have done this in my business, and maybe how you can find out about failing businesses in your sector. Well, it's all about building a network and selling yourself as the person to do this in your field. I always make sure I am known for this in my sector. I always offer to speak free of charge at industry events and conferences - this tactic has got me in front of thousands of people who might be in trouble in the future, or indeed may want to sell up now. I have always seized any opportunity for the trade or general press to write stories about me, so if a bank or finance company has a business on its books that's facing trouble they call me up and offer me the business, and I negotiate terms.

Being in the know for your sector means you can be the first contact for opportunities that come up. You could even write to people you know are in trouble and say that you may be interested in their business - you could be the answer to their prayers.

Lastly, if a business that interests you has been up for sale for a long time without selling, it may be the time to explore the possibility of a buyout.

Timing is everything with businesses you buy because they're in trouble. It could be a forced closure, perhaps through a landlord who's got the hump because the rent hasn't been paid, or a bank with late loan repayments. But for you as the buyer, the profit is made by buying at the right price. If you can buy a business for £50k that will be worth £500k two years down the line once you have sorted it out, that's a nice profit. It's not so good if you pay £500k and sell it for the same amount - this happens, believe me.

You need to know when the time is right for your cash flow and operation. Over stretching at the wrong time could quickly turn you too into a failing business - this has happened to so many business owners.

Know why it's failing - don't become the next failure

When looking at distressed businesses sales, you need to understand what got the business into trouble. Is it because no one wants the service or product? If so, walk away, because nothing can be done here - no cure, I'm afraid. Is it just bad management, or perhaps the owner has had enough? In that case, get in and implement the rules of my book - inject energy and get results. My favourite one is when the business is over-leveraged with too many costs which it cannot meet, yet it actually turns good money. The latter is gold dust, because for me in an established trading business I can negotiate all the costs out of the business by bringing them into the costs we already pay, so we get economies of scale. We could use the same marketing, accounts and head office team, for example. More importantly, overheads like rents may be sky high because the original owner set the business up without enough knowledge or basic understanding of costs or overheads. If the business has premises and is going to go bust, chances are it will lease premises, as the landlord will not want to lose a tenant. I would say 60% of the time the landlord will reduce the rent when he knows a tenant will go bust or is in financial difficulty - I know this because I have done this every time I have taken over a business. I have always negotiated the rent down on the premises when the landlord thinks 'if I don't let this guy take over my property, it will be empty and I'll get no rent at all.'

Every time I have done this I have told the landlord, 'Look, I need a sizeable rent-free period, a minimum of six months but preferably two years to sort this business out, because it's in trouble and needs my help to sort it, otherwise it's game over'. In fact I am prepared to walk away if the deal is not agreed. Then I get the actual rent down by a minimum of 40% each time as well.

In some premises the fit-out or equipment and vehicles for the business could be owed to finance companies or banks via loans which the company could not afford to service - time for you to negotiate again. In my experience when things like this happen finance houses turn from 'how much can we make?' to 'what's the least we can lose?' This will allow you to do a deal for a percentage in the pound for the equipment, saving more on business set-up costs.

All of the above I have done over and over, but I have walked away from deals too, because my demands for the long-term health of the business could not be matched. I know I need low overheads.

Funny thing is, I walked away from a deal in Oxford when an operator went bust because the landlord wanted too much rent for his site and the fixtures he had seized on failure of rent payment, so he gave it to another operator who had just started. They went bust within two years. The landlord then called me up and said 'OK James, let's talk on your terms'. Two years on, the site is successful. We are the operators and the landlord gets his rent paid with a guarantee from me.

You have to be fair on these deals. A little wiggle room is allowed on the terms you have set yourself, but not too much. Just because you can pick something up cheap doesn't mean it's without its troubles, so negotiate the lowest fair price possible.

I am not in the business of doing people over, so I have always offered company guarantees and PGs whilst I have been the operator of a site, to give comfort to landlords and banks I am negotiating with. Lots of business owners won't do this. I can understand why not, but deals need to be done and something will have to be offered to the other side to achieve this. Offering a deposit for a year or a PG for a certain period of time will give people like banks and landlords peace of mind.

TOP TIP

As a rule I like to have no more than 20% of my turnover as debt. It's not an accurate science but this approach will keep you safe. Being cautious with debt is important. You need debt to grow - but not too much!

16.
COMPETE ON EXPERIENCE, NOT PRICE

A lot of business people fret about price. Is my service/product too cheap? Is it too expensive? Correct pricing really drives a business, as in many ways the price dictates who you are. Lots of businesses seem to think people buy only on price. That's simply not true, BUT - it's true that people will only pay more than they have to IF they're getting a good experience in return. Even rich people want value for money - trust me!

Small start-up businesses often say 'If I could just could get a couple of blue chip clients, that would make us'. They assume a blue chip will have plenty of money and spend large sums without a second thought. Yet the blue chips still have just as a cunning an eye for value as small companies - after all, how did they get to be blue chips?

Some big, wealthy companies will aggressively drive down prices with every supplier because that's the culture that's developed from the top down, while some small businesses will take the view that they want their suppliers to do well out of a deal and be happy partners, and they'll want to pay them fairly, knowing they are likely to get better loyalty and service.

As I said earlier, systems and processes will be in place to get the best value for money, but if you push experience, customers will often pay a 30% premium over the competition to get the pain resolved and still won't think it's expensive. They will say the magic line, 'OK it's a bit more expensive, but it's worth the money'. Remember Apple!

Don't get caught in the trap of competing on price because you need to turn over more to get the profits you want. Through my networking I met two bosses from the UK's biggest supermarket chains. When we got chatting, I learned that they work to 3% profit margins. You need to turn over a huge amount to make a million-pound profit on 3% - but of course, they do turn over huge amounts. Working with turnovers of billions of pounds is another game entirely and not one I'm qualified to talk about. What I do know is that all supermarkets constantly battle for market share, and they do this by competing on price.

If you chase low pricing and become cheap, you can't hope to deliver experience and service of a high standard, and these are things people are happy to pay for. Some supermarkets do deliver experience and service, but only through economies of scale and heavy investment in training and systems.

Nothing matters more than customer service. People talk about B2B and B2C businesses, but really it should be H2H - human to human. People who become customers of any of the Partyman businesses love our facilities, love our offer, but above all they love our team, love our ways, love our people. When you manage to get great people in your team, you will achieve high customer retention and repeat business will fly through the door (this is hard to do and takes effort). That means you don't need to market so aggressively. Your customers will do a lot of it for you. People will happily pay 20-30% more to you than they will to your competitors if the service you deliver makes you value for money. And it's a whole lot easier for small businesses to do this - in fact as you get bigger, you will find it gets harder to do it. It just needs to be worked on daily. The easy way is to have lots of systems and process that work. I am no fan of time-wasting rules and systems - only good ones that make a difference.

Don't forget you still need to market your experience, no matter how busy you are - the tap must always stay on, but it's a lot easier to market an experience-led business that customers love. How easy have Apple got it? They push the *experience* the product gives rather than the product itself. They have consistently delivered on this, so people have bought into the brand, and a brand means trust. This trust means that when they launch a product people queue up for it the day before it goes on sale because they trust the brand to deliver consistent excellence.

So it's experience that can make you a sector leader. My favourite restaurant in sunny Essex, Alvaro's, looks like my Nan's front room, but just you try and get a table there. The waiters and owners make it an experience, and the food is melt-in-the-mouth, but the place has old furniture and I really don't think they have ever had a refurb. Even so, I can't think of many experience-led businesses that are so aesthetically pleasing, and it gives the business character - character is experience too, the character makes it feel good.

So what makes an experience for a business, one that will save you having to compete on price?

Aesthetics

In my opinion aesthetics are a tool in the bag for building an experience for customers, even if it's just your offices and toilets. If you're a dentist then the entrance waiting room and reception need to offer the right experience. Theming, good decor, natural light and good signage all contribute to the make-up. It sounds obvious, but people love it.

Feel and character

I believe the ambience of a business does add to the experience of it all, the feeling you get when you arrive - for example great uniforms, clean shoes, team members in good form with positive body language, cleanliness, the right smell, clean windows, a nice atmosphere, open space. But what if when you arrive at the dentist the floor is dirty, the staff in reception are unhelpful and the dentist has jeans and a polo shirt on? It just doesn't feel right.

Our staff have amazing uniforms, with a positive body language and attitude. I want a nice smell and the place should be airy, bright and with just the right level of music.

Shock and awe

Under-promising and then over-delivering is the trick to get this one in the bag. Some businesses seem to bombard their customers with every promise under the sun – they'll pay your mortgage off and improve your sex life too! Much better not to tell your customers everything you will do for them. Then when you surprise them with something they were not expecting, they are awed and delighted by the experience. It's the little things that make this happen.

To deliver this, give them something free which they were expecting to pay for. If you run a restaurant, you could add a little extra to the dishes that's not in the menu description or when a customer does business with you, send them a hand-written thank you card - who does that nowadays? Just create a little extra love and warmth to get the experience across.

Consistency

Consistency of experience delivery is what you need to master – in fact you need to live by it. Don't become that restaurant that has a fab opening, but when customers go back the food isn't quite so good, the people are ill-trained, service is slow and it's all rather a disappointment. Keep the experience consistent, not up one week and down the next. System and process will help with this.

Why is McDonalds the biggest restaurant chain in the world? Because they offer a consistent experience of their product. McDonalds is a price-led business selling meals cheap and relying on volume - not for me, thanks.

People deliver experience by using the right vocal tonality. They need to look and sound like experts, with great body language, build rapport with customers and offer exceptional service.

Your people will shine if they love the same three things as your customers - the product, the people and the experience.

To create customers for life, you need to keep the experience consistent. You can't be an experience-led business today then not tomorrow, or it's game over.

When things go wrong

Having said all that, you can't guarantee that every customer experience will be good. From time to time something will go wrong with the service you give your customers, even in the best-run business – a contaminated restaurant meal, an order that never turns up, the wrong furniture delivered, a final demand sent to someone who has died. When it does, it's all the more important to make this a good experience for customers. It's actually an OPPORTUNITY to shine by showing how much you care. If you can repair and compensate for the damage properly, they will love you even more than they did before.

Businesses that compete on experience don't have to worry half as much as price-led businesses. They have much more loyal fan bases, with a recession-proof bunch of customers who are not just looking for the cheapest option.

When I was a full-time children's entertainer, I charged more and did more, yet I got away without marketing or advertising – it all happened because I was competing on experience. Competition will creep up behind you in your sector, but by competing on experience you will protect yourself. Your rivals will try to copy the experience you provide, but can they keep it consistent? Consistency is the key for longevity.

Some key points to note

Always offer exceptional value for money, but that does not mean being cheap.

Remember businesses that compete on price have very little margin movement and usually low profit to turn over. It's much better to make a profit of 20% on a lower turnover than 2.5% on a massive turnover.

Experience-led businesses are the ones that get super-loyal customers that love you and are prepared to give referrals and testimonials.

People will pay a margin for a great experience, which means easier profits for you - and if they won't pay for that, do you want them as customers?

If you think they won't, look at coffee shops now. Gone are the greasy spoon and the faded department store café and hello to sofas and relaxing music, with an average spend per head of £6 for a cup of coffee and a slice of cake. The new coffee shops are everywhere, yet where were they 15 years ago?

17.
SEIZE OPPORTUNITIES

Let's start this last chapter with the subject of opportunity. It comes knocking on all our doors in life, some more often than others, but I firmly believe opportunity comes to those who want it most. It's been said before, but I also believe that the harder you work and the more you put yourself out, the luckier you get.

Unless you have inherited opportunity or wealth, the thing I love about life is that we all start from zero and we all get served opportunities along the way. It's the entrepreneurs who seize those opportunities and make them happen for the good of the rest of us. Imagine the nasty things people like Mark Zuckerberg, Bill Gates and the Google founders could have done with the power they have. Between them they control the biggest companies in the world with serious cash - ultimately they all want to do well.

Simply put, I seize and will continue to seize all the opportunities that come knocking on my door, and so should you. If you want to be an entrepreneur who moves mountains, get moving. Fear is something that hold lots of people back.

When I was 23, I found myself talking to the richest man I've ever met; he was worth around £70 million. His name was Charles. I asked him, 'How did you become so successful and so happy?' Before I tell you the answer he gave me, let me explain just what this guy was about. He was elderly, cultured and very smart. Next to his desk were pictures of various prime ministers of years gone by who he had dined with. There was a picture of him with his dogs in his own helicopter.

The meeting was in his study, and it looked like something from a stately home (actually it *was* a stately home), set in his own country estate in acres of beautiful English countryside. Charles might have been posh, but he was also down to earth and had his ear as firmly to the ground as any man I had met. He told me he had just got back from his estate in South Africa, and went on to tell me a story about how he had landed his helicopter on his golf club's roof! Charles loved swear words and every other word began with an F, but he managed to do it with such style that it never seemed vulgar.

Charles was a pleasure to deal with, so much so that we bought the freehold of one of his properties and traded from it. He made the deal simple, fair and easy to do - it was a breeze, because he just decided there and then how to do it.

So why is this all relevant? Because his answer really shook my thinking. It was simply this: *Don't be too fucking clever!*

Those were his exact words. They hit me like a tidal wave. He was right, of course - if you try to think like an accountant, a solicitor or a banker you will miss the opportunities in life. Hard work and vision are what you need.

He has sadly passed on now, but Charles, I always have followed your advice. I would always take risks and give it a go, but you made it a key rule for getting things done and making things happen. Remember always to take calculated risks and protect the downside at all times. Fail gracefully and learn when things go wrong. Things will always go wrong, but that's OK as long as you know to make them go right again and know *why* you went wrong.

Furthermore, this man knew his 'why' - he wanted to make money, but I like to think his 'why' was simply that he wanted to enjoy his life to the full, and to me that's a good enough 'why' if I heard one. (He also loved dogs - and I love a furry mutt too, if I have a weak spot for anything, it's dogs.)

When things get tough, as they will, when cashflow gets hit, as it will, when times get stressful, as they will, if you know why you're doing it, it's so much easier to tackle the problem. Succession planning and knowing what the business is doing is an essential part of what you do as a leader or business owner. You are the objective setter, and if you're doing well then you will implement and execute the strategies with your team, because no successful entrepreneur is a one-man army.

Make sure you know how the business is going to go on ticking away without you. It's a responsibility you have to your team and your customers - as soon as you employ people, you become responsible for their livelihood. It's prudent to make sure you plan for things go on working in your absence should you fall ill or get run over by a bus - or simply go on holiday.

I love what I do, and I love the friends I have made in business. I enjoy watching competition come up which raises industry standards, which further improves us and helps the consumer. Then in turn we have to do more to be leaders in each sector we operate.

Lastly, if you have a business, I believe that every year you get older you should think about the effect it will have on you as an individual. How much of your life is your business taking up? Do you enjoy it? Don't forget that all-important point from our first rules - why are you doing it?

Many may think entrepreneurs and successful people just do it for the money, but I do it because – well, because I like doing it. To me money is a source of energy to allow me to do things and if that ever stops, that's the day I need to change. A business should fund a lifestyle for you and your family, but it should also give you happiness and a sense of worth, a feeling that what you are doing is good - at least, that's what I believe.

We entrepreneurs are a funny breed of people. For us, work is not work – it's a necessary part of the makeup of who we are. One thing that sets me apart - and writing this book has made me realise this more than anything – is this: if you're happy inside, you can take so much more on. That's why, at the top of all my life goal lists, is 'I am happy inside'. Life seemed pointless until I had mastered this point. Having a great home life, being in love and enjoying yourself is so important. I am now completely happy inside, and it makes me eager to take on much more.

You see my business, like so many, was an upward struggle in the early years, and it's fair to say I was sailing close to the wind at times. But if you feel happy inside and you have a strong, loving relationship with the key person in your life, then life is so much easier. If you are single, make sure your family and your friends are there for you.

It's also vital to get the right balance between your work and your personal life. I certainly got this wrong at first. As I said earlier, time is a vital commodity - you can always get material things back, but you can never get your time back. The seven days a week I used to do, every week for 10 years, was not a good idea. I now only ever work a six-day week maximum. I love work, but I have finally discovered 'James time'. I used to think holidays and time off were a waste of time, but they certainly are not! Enjoy your life.

I plan to carry on building Partyman as my first true love in business, but I also want to help people into business by talking at seminars and telling my story at events so I can help people and share my ideas. Through this book I am launching my new business, 'James Sinclair's Entrepreneurs Network', with high-energy seminars, monthly facts, nuggets and business gold for all our members to help people to become super successful. To find out more click on www.jamessinclair.net. I am also still entertaining and public speaking whenever I can. For some reason people like to know how a clown built up a multi-million pound business from scratch in his twenties! This, my first book, is just the start, so I can give something to people to take away. I have to admit I also love standing in front of people and doing my thing on stage. Some people have a fear of being on stage - I have a fear of *not* being on stage!

I am fortunate enough to live on Marsh Farm, nestling in the beautiful Essex countryside with our 400 animals, my dog Boris and cat Mogbat. I also have a wonderful girlfriend, Natalie, and at the time of writing we have just started a recruitment business which she is running - not fun enough for me! This is great for me as I won't have anything to do with the day-to-day running, but I'll get to see the running of a business that's in a completely new sector. We have a roof over our heads and plenty of holidays, and hopefully one day in the not-too-distant future some mini-Jimbos enjoying life to the full.

I have already been wealthy for half my life because I have loved, been healthy, made people laugh and laughed lots myself. I've had a go, done what I wanted and fed myself with whatever I need, and I'm still only 29. If you really look at your life you are already wealthy, in some ways - maybe you just need more money or 'energy' to fulfil the vision you have set.

Don't forget folks, money is energy and all you need to succeed in getting the bigger dreams you have in life is a little more energy. Just always know your 'why', because money has no meaning without it. If you don't know your 'why', you will never be happy, and happiness is what it's all about.

I hope my book helps you in your life journey and business success.

THE MILLIONAIRE CLOWN

Magically Yours

A very happy

James JIMBO Sinclair

Chief Clown
Founder of The Partyman Group and having a laugh.

PS: My thanks to all the wonderful people I have met in my life, my family and friends, to Aaron and all my wonderful team who have been with me over the years we have worked together and helped me to build a company that grows every year. I mean that from the bottom of my bottom. I love you all!

James Sinclair's
Entrepreneurs network

If you enjoyed my book and are hungry for more, then don't worry! You can come and meet me at one of my FREE Business Growth Seminars.

To find out the latest dates of all my seminars visit www.jamessinclair.net

Or email me at hello@jamessinclair.net or you can call a member of my team on 08450 345 111